How to g

How to get an MBA is a short study guide for prospective MBA students wanting to know more about what is involved, for students in a new intake at a business school and for those seeking to prepare themselves for the experience to come.

Topics covered include how to:

- work in teams
- communicate effectively in classrooms
- develop and manage personal networks
- read and prepare a case
- present written material
- design and carry out a project
- use library information sources
- look for a job at the end of the course.

The book shows students how to make the most of their MBA experience and how to make it work for them in the future.

Morgen Witzel is an independent writer, editor and lecturer. He is author of the *Dictionary of Business and Management* and, with Tim Ambler, of *Doing Business in China*.

How to get an MBA

Morgen Witzel

London and New York

First published 2000 by Routledge
11 New Fetter Lane, London EC4P 4EE

Simultaneously published in the USA and Canada
by Routledge
29 West 35th Street, New York, NY 10001

Routledge is an imprint of the Taylor & Francis Group

Typset in Palatino by The Midlands Book Typesetting Company, Loughborough, Leics.
Printed and bound in Great Britain by TJ International Ltd, Padstow, Cornwall.

British Library Cataloguing in Publication Data
A Catalogue record for this book is available from the British Library

Library of Congress Cataloging in Publication Data
Witzel, Morgen.
  How to get an MBA / Morgen Witzel.
    p. cm.
  Includes bibliographical references and index.
  ISBN 0-415-22817-4
  1. Master of business administration degree. 2. Business education. 3. Industrial
management--Study and teaching (Graduate) I. Title.

HF1111 .W58 2001
650'.071'173--dc21

                                                          00-056024

ISBN 0-415-22817-4

Contents

Acknowledgements

This book is the product of many people's experiences, and I am grateful to the faculty, staff and students of the various business schools with which I have had dealings over the past ten years. Their names are too many to mention here, but I would like to add a special mention to the faculty and students of the China–Europe International Business School in Shanghai who made me so welcome on my visit there.

Valuable comments on the original proposal came from George Bickerstaffe and Gay Haskins, and my thanks to them both. Thomas Wood added a couple of late suggestions. Marilyn Livingstone has, as ever, been my greatest supporter and helper.

Most special thanks, however, must go to Nina Stibbe, who commissioned this book, and to Jude Bowen who worked with me for much of the writing process. Their confidence and support have made this book possible. My thanks too to Julia Swales and Anna Clarkson at Routledge.

Finally, I would like to thank Basil Hone for his superb illustrations, which I hope will make pleasant reading, even for those who don't approve of the book.

Introduction

The MBA is perhaps the most talked about and discussed form of management education in the world. Despite its venerable age (the first MBA degrees were awarded in the early twentieth century), MBA programmes remain both popular and relevant. Although critics of the programmes have been numerous, large companies and increasingly small ones as well continue to see real value in the MBA as the first stage in a professional career in management.

This book assumes that the reader has already made up his or her mind to do an MBA, and probably chosen and been accepted by a business school as well; indeed, the programme may already have started. It is aimed equally at full-time, part-time, executive and distance learning MBAs, although some parts of the book will obviously be of more or less relevance, depending on what programme the reader is joining.

The first important point is that there is no 'one way' to get an MBA degree. There is no road map to success here, any more than there is in the rest of a manager's career (or life); tempting though it may be to assume that there is.

Any idea that there should be such a simple solution must be dispelled as soon as we begin to consider MBA programmes themselves. Though they often have very similar curricula and aims, MBA programmes are certainly not homogeneous. Many programmes differ in terms of aims, philosophies and teaching/delivery methods. Even more importantly, though, MBA students are a very diverse bunch. Walking through the campus of any leading business school, one will encounter people from many different countries, backgrounds and professions.

Gone are the days – if they ever existed – when the mere possession of an MBA degree was enough to secure for the degree holder a rosy future at the top level of a large corporation, complete with large salary and generous perks. Many MBA students, to be sure, *do* graduate into such jobs. Others don't. The initials MBA no longer have the pulling power they did thirty years ago. Corporate recruiters no longer take the MBA degree itself as a guarantee of quality. They look for many other factors, including:

- the school from which the degree was granted
- the programme which the graduate is attending or has attended
- what practical experience the graduate may have gained while on the programme

and, most important of all,

- the personal qualities of the graduate, including evidence of personal development while on the programme

Increasingly, companies are looking generally, at the qualities of the institution, and specifically, at the individual graduate and his or her qualities. In other words, they are not looking for the MBA degree, but for the *quality of the person who has it*.

Many roads to the same end

During the 1980s and 1990s there arose a proliferation of different models of MBA programmes: full-time and part-time, day and evening, distance learning MBAs, executive MBAs (of which there are at least a dozen different definitions), MBAs specializing in finance, marketing, information management or other business disciplines, MBAs specializing in European or Asian business, and so on and on. All these are really just alternative delivery means to the same end.

I should make it clear at the outset that the issues discussed here are ones which affect all MBA students, regardless of the kind of programme they are engaged in. The desirable end product – a confident, capable person capable of taking on the heavy tasks of senior management – remains the same.

Getting an MBA degree, therefore, is ultimately about developing yourself, improving your own personal qualities and improving your ability to manage. This applies whether the student is looking to change jobs or career paths, seek advancement within a firm for which they already work, or start their own business. *How to Get an MBA*, then, is a book which suggests ways in which students can *maximize the value* of the MBA experience.

The MBA is a once-in-a-lifetime experience. It is, or can be, extremely expensive in terms of money and time. For most who go on such programmes, it is a life-changing experience. In order to maximize the value of the MBA, students need to look beyond the basics of classroom learning, important though these are, and consider such issues as

- gaining practical experience
- developing networks and relationships
- developing communications and interpersonal skills
- broadening personal horizons
- learning how to learn

Now more than ever, it is important to get an MBA not just for the degree itself, but for the *experience*. The diploma hanging on your wall at the end of the programme is no more than a sheet of paper. What is important that comes out of the MBA is what is in your *mind*. One of the most important concepts which this book introduces is the concept of the MBA as primarily a learning experience. The important benefits of the MBA include not just the knowledge that one absorbs while on the programme, but the necessary learning skills that accompany this. The two are combined in a single system which we refer to here as *knowledge management*.

The MBA only happens once. You will never be on this programme again. You may never again have this opportunity to learn – although, as is argued later in the book, the MBA is a first step in a process of lifelong learning, and this is a formulative learning experience. The ideas and skills you gain here will affect your personal and professional life forever after.

This is a highly personal and subjective book, and I make no apology for that. Its origins are to be found in a deep belief in the value of the MBA as an incubator for managerial talent, and

SOMEDAY SON, AFTER YOUR MBA STUDIES, ALL THIS WILL BE YOURS

an almost equal concern that some of those who embark on MBA programmes do not always extract the maximum possible value from the experience. Talent must not be wasted; the world is too short of it already. If this book helps even a few people emerge from MBA programmes with greater skills and abilities than they might otherwise have done, then it will have succeeded in its aims.

Chapter 1

Learning how to learn

You read a book from beginning to end. You run a business the opposite way. You start with the end, and then do everything you must to
reach it.
Harold Geneen

Before getting into the MBA programme proper, it is first necessary to devote some time to the fundamental ideas on which this
book is based. In particular, there are two important processes
that go on all during the MBA programme. The first, which we
have already referred to, is *benefit maximization*. The second, more
practical process, is *knowledge management*. To consider how these
work and are related, consider the following six points:

1   Education is a service. Every student has some *input* into the
     education they receive. What you take out depends in part
     on what you put in.
2   Every MBA student will have a set of personal and career
     goals, what they hope to achieve from the programme. These
     will help to shape the learning experience.
3   Every MBA programme offers a series of core *benefits*, which
     are built into the design of the programme.
4   Depending on the student's goals (2), he or she can work to
     maximize the benefits (3) he or she receives from the
     programme, and this in turn will help to define more clearly
     his or her own input (1) into the programme.

5 Once this picture is clear, the student can then work out what *resources* are needed, developing a 'resource-based' view of the MBA programme.
6 Finally, from this basis, the student can define a *knowledge management strategy* which will enable maximization to occur.

Figure 1.1 below shows how these elements interrelate. The student begins by assessing the *benefits* of the programme in light of his or her personal and career *goals*, and then works out how to *maximize* those benefits. (The maximization process can help to further define those goals, hence this is shown as a circular

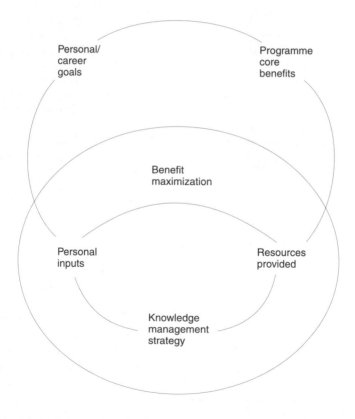

Figure 1.1 Relating goals and motivations to resources and strategy

process.) Maximization is in turn a circular process; the *resources* provided by the programme combine with personal *inputs* to develop a knowledge maximization strategy; and, as this develops, so the types and levels of resources needed can change (hence this too is shown as a circular process)

This is probably about as clear as mud. Don't worry too much; the chapters which follow should make it clear how this works. The main theme, put more simply, is to focus on goals and then work out how to get the most out of the MBA programme to propel you towards those goals.

When should all this happen?

Ideally, of course, you will have had a chance to work all this out in advance, before the programme starts. You will be clear about your goals, and you will have a good idea of the benefits of the programme. You will know what resources are available, and you will have some idea of what you will need to put into the programme. Thus you can begin to design the two loops, benefit maximization and knowledge management.

But conditions are seldom ideal, and there is every chance that you will need to do a lot of this in the early stages of the programme. Chapter 2, getting started, deals with the vital first few days of any MBA programme.

Education and the service process

In education, as in all services, the quality of the service depends to some extent on the consumer. To use the jargon of the services marketing experts, 'the consumer is part of the production process'. When we go to restaurants, for example, we make choices from the menu, interact with the staff and sometimes other customers, consume the food and wine we have ordered and so on. We do not passively accept what the staff provide us (well, not in most restaurants, at least), we are part of the process.

So it is with education. Learning is not a passive process; one cannot simply sit in a classroom and let knowledge transfer from lecturer to student through some form of osmosis. We learn through interacting with others, lecturers and staff, fellow students and so on. Our willingness to learn, our learning skills (listening, analysing, communicating, etc.) and our personal goals and needs all have an impact on *what* we learn and *how* we learn it.

Real learning is an active process. It involves questioning information which is found in lectures, textbooks and cases and so on, and analysing it for value. It involves seeking out resources and people who may have information or knowledge which can be of use. It involves learning from real-life, everyday situations, not just in formal settings.

Learning is not about absorbing information. It is about gathering and using knowledge. The importance of the student's own role in this process cannot be overemphasized. No matter how good the teaching materials, no matter how high the quality of the lecturers, one has responsibility for one's own learning.

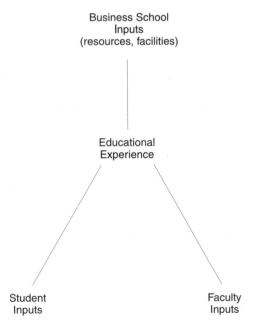

Figure 1.2 The service production process in education

Further information

If the reader is coming from a background in services marketing, then much of the above will already sound familiar. If not, and if the explanations given here are insufficient, then there are several good books on services marketing which go into these concepts in more detail. Recommended for novice readers are John E.G. Bateson and K. Douglas Hoffman, *Managing Services Marketing* (Fort Worth, TX: Dryden, 1999) and L.L. Berry and A. Parasuraman, *Marketing Services: Competing Through Quality* (New York: The Free Press, 1991).

Setting and defining goals

Everyone enters an MBA programme with his or her own highly personal set of goals. Generally, though, each of these goals falls into one of two categories:

- professional, which usually means advancing one's career, changing careers, getting a better job, or starting one's own business
- personal, usually relating to self-development, vision and so on, and possibly also including developing personal and interpersonal skills such as communication and networking

There isn't really much more to be said on this subject (this is a rather obvious point anyway), except to acknowledge that most people's goals are complex rather than simple, and likely include elements of both categories above. And in fact, a mix of the two is by far the healthiest option. A concentration on the professional over the personal can lead to a narrow-mindedness and lack of vision that can compromise rather than assist professional advancement. Similarly, too much focus on the personal and not enough on the professional can result in a well-rounded person with a great vision – and no job.

Me? A student?

In the 1990s there arose a prejudice against referring to people taking MBA programmes as 'students'. It was felt that 'student' referred to undergraduates, and was not appropriate to mature, experienced people. Calling MBA programme members students was seen as an affront to their dignity.

But 'participants', the fashionable alternative, implies a distance between the people and the programme. Other options are not much better. And anyway, is it such a bad thing to be a student?

The *Oxford English Dictionary* defines a student as 'a person studying in order to qualify himself or herself for some occupation, or devoting himself or herself to some branch of learning or investigation.' To me, this seems a highly appropriate term for people on MBA programmes, and I shall therefore refer to them as 'students' throughout this book.

Core benefits

The benefits offered by MBA programmes are complex and variable, but most programmes offer at least some of the following, and many offer most or all:

- *skills development*, including acquiring new skills and improving existing ones. This benefit is especially valuable for students coming in from a fairly narrow functional background (marketing, finance, HRM, etc.) and seeking either a change in career path or a broad package of skills suitable for general management.
- *global vision*, or more specifically, learning to work, live and manage in the global marketplace. Globalization is a bit like electricity; everyone sees its effects, but rather fewer people know how it works. Global experience and outlook is seen as an important benefit of many programmes.
- *a broader outlook*, or in general terms, learning to look outside one's own firm, business sector, business function and so on and to develop a greater appreciation of how firms, functions, markets and so on interact. Schopenhauer once wrote that 'every man takes the limits of his own field of vision as the limits of the world'. Breaking out of this way of thinking leads to the next benefit,

- *integrated thinking*, or learning how to visualize both the whole *and* the interaction of the parts, whether in terms of firms, markets, business systems or whatever. This is seen as one of the most important components of management today, and also of such concepts as creativity and innovation. This also includes seeing oneself as a part of a system, networking, team management and so on.

- *preparation for leadership*, acquiring both the skills and the mindset necessary to be a successful leader of an organization. Confidence, decision-making ability and communications skills, for example, are seen as essential ingredients.

- *knowledge management*, the latest addition to the list. Still something of a buzzword (do most of the people who talk about knowledge management really know what it is?), the term 'knowledge management' nevertheless encompasses some important concepts. It is generally accepted that in the post-industrial economies of the west, knowledge has become one of the most important resources and commodities; there is talk of 'knowledge capital', which joins finance capital and labour as one of the key factors of production. Learning to manage organizational knowledge, therefore, is seen as being a key benefit. (There is also the issue of managing your own, personal knowledge, which we return to below.)

Again, this may be obvious to most readers, but it is worth rehearsing these benefits and identifying where and how these (and any others) appear in the programme one is taking before moving on to look at benefit maximization.

Maximizing benefits

We have been throwing this term around for a few pages now, and it is time to determine exactly what it means:

Maximizing benefits means achieving the maximum possible during the course of an MBA programme, in terms of both personal development and career potential.

The MBA is, as mentioned above, a life-changing experience; use it to the full. More pragmatically, the MBA is likely to be expensive in terms of money, time or both; you owe it to yourself to get the greatest possible value in return for your investment.

This is, of course, easier said than done. The argument here is that the best way to maximize value is to treat the MBA as a service process, as outlined above. It follows, then, that the first step is to get to know the components of that process and how they will fit together to provide the service.

It must be emphasized again that what we are talking about here is *active learning*, in which the student actively *seeks out* source of knowledge, *makes opportunities* for learning, and is receptive to information and knowledge from a *broad range of sources*. It must be emphasized too that this is not a mindset that one needs to develop solely for the MBA. Exactly this approach to learning will be called for throughout one's subsequent career.

Another way of characterizing this concept might be to call it an *entrepreneurial approach to learning*. Part of the learning process is a constant, often subconcious scanning of the environment for opportunities for learning, and an assessment of knowledge gained in terms of its potential present or future usefulness. In other words, you are not just gathering knowledge for its own sake, you are treating it like a personal asset. This might be a useful concept to remember when structuring your own knowledge management programme (below).

There is a final point which needs to be made, and this concerns the *individual nature of learning*. One of the fascinating things about human cognition, and one of the things that separates us from computers, is its individual nature; every one of us sees things differently. The differences may be imperceptible, or they may be vast, yawning gulfs. Put ten computers in a room and input a set of data into each, and you will get the same output from each (assuming, of course, that each is loaded with the same software, and each has been installed correctly, and IT haven't accidentally deleted a key driver from the second machine on the end). Put ten people in a room, especially ten people from different cultural, educational and technical backgrounds and ask them to describe an ordinary object, and you may get ten quite different responses. (This is one of the things that makes teamworking so fascinating; see Chapter 5.)

THE MBA APPLICANT IS HERE TO INTERVIEW YOU

What this boils down to is that *each learning experience is unique*. How you learn is quite different from how your neighbour learns. Each of you will sit through the same lecture or work on the same case study, yet your cognitive processes will work differently, and you will take away different bits of information and analyse them to produce different kinds of knowledge. Although several hundred people may be involved in taking the same programme, attending lectures by the same faculty and writing up the same case studies, *each graduate will be a unique product*.

And this in turn puts personal and career goals – the motivation for taking an MBA in the first place – under scrutiny. The MBA programme offers the chance to shape your own life and career in a way that will make you unique and different, to stand out from the crowd, to be a star. It can mark you out as someone with intelligence, ability, potential. Are your goals in line with your potential? Now is the time to ask.

What do recruiters look for in an MBA?

The last two or three decades have seen something of a change in what corporate recruiters expect to find in an MBA candidate. In the 1950s and 1960s, in terms of the core benefits above, the emphasis was strongly on skills and leadership qualities; integrated thinking and global vision were less regarded, if at all. Today the situation has changed, and qualities of vision and thinking are regarded as as important, in some cases more important, than pure skills.

In part the change has occurred because of changes in the world economy, with globalization and the importance of knowledge as a commodity (referred to above) increasing in profile. But also, the MBA is no longer regarded as an automatic ticket to high office; instead, it is seen as a first step on a path of career-long learning (see Chapter 13).

Recruiters, then, are looking for potential. With this in mind, the MBA can be seen not as opportunity for great achievements, but as a chance to develop one's own *potential* to achieve great things.

A resource-based view of the MBA programme

As mentioned above, the first step in determining how to maximize benefits is to determine what resources are available. Generally speaking, resources fall into four categories:

- data and information repositiories
- the business school's faculty
- other students
- oneself

Data and information repositories

These include books, journals, CD-ROMs, websites and other sources of data and information, whether located in the business school's library or elsewhere. This is in some ways the easiest resource to manage, as it is possible to control and order the information needed; although managing information sources, particularly those found on the Internet, can be seen as a skill in its own right. The main features of this category of resource are:

- comprehensiveness; no one knows just how many billions of words have been written and statistics compiled about management and business since the beginning of time, but in theory at least, if you want to know something, you can almost certainly find it.
- it includes sources of both hard data and ideas; this is where to go if you want hard data, but you can also find any number of varying ideas on any given theme, and comparing these can help broaden your own outlook.
- it is essentially passive; statistics, books and articles are always there, so you can manage your use of them to suit your time. Various indices and search engines can usually help to sift through the mass of information and data available to focus your search. On the other hand, you cannot get involved in a dialogue with them; in the learning process, it is you who have to do all the work.

These resources are also discussed in Chapter 8.

Business school faculty

Business school faculty have many tasks and priorities, but from the student's point of view, their principal function is to deliver information and knowledge to students. How they do this depends on personal style and also on the philosophy of the institution which employs them. Thirty years ago, most business school faculty worked in the classic 'teacher' mode, delivering lectures to students and imparting knowledge directly to them, rather as most undergraduate teaching continues to do. This is sometimes known as the 'chalk and talk' method. More recently, the trend has been for faculty to be 'guides', helping students to learn rather than teaching 'at' them. In fact, most faculty opt for a combination of methods, depending on circumstances, the subject being discussed, the ability of the class and so on.

The method is actually rather less important than the objective. If the best method for learning happens to be direct teaching, so be it; if it is case studies, project work or group discussions, then these will be employed. The point of faculty is that they are channels through which knowledge – often highly specialized knowledge which might be difficult to track down and assimilate through other sources – is directed at the student. One definition of 'faculty', to quote the *Oxford English Dictionary* once more, is 'an aptitude or competence for any special kind of action'. Faculty, then, are specialist repositories of knowledge with the additional ability of being able to guide students through the learning process. They are the ultimate in interactive learning.

In some types of programme, such as distance learning MBAs, contact with faculty may be restricted. Most, such as the Open University's distance learning MBA based in the UK, do have arrangements for faculty contact. Some newer programmes are opting for electronic methods such as computer-assisted learning, in which faculty input is mediated through the teaching software. This has obvious practical advantages, but can be less satisfying (obviously) in terms of interaction. (Why is that help menus on these programmes never have the answer to the question you really need to ask?)

The main features of this category of resource are:

- intelligent agents; unlike passive information repositories, faculty can structure and restructure knowledge to make it easy to understand and analyse. The constant interaction between faculty and students means that the learning process tends to be faster and more efficient. However, being human (well, more or less), there are greater limits to the knowledge that any individual member of faculty can be expected to possess. Therefore, they have a second key function, that of

- guide; one thing about faculty members is that even if they don't know the answer to a question, they are usually fairly sure of where to go to look it up. One well-directed question can often save hours of looking through indexes or trawling through search programme results on the Internet.

- specialist expertise; faculty members have specialist knowledge of their areas of research and interest, and this can be an especially valuable source of knowledge. Each faculty member will have a unique combination of research interests, and this in turn gives them a unique perspective on some aspect of management. This is a resource which should not be overlooked.

- independence of mind; their position in a business school, a little outside the mainstream of business affairs, means they have no particular axe to grind when it comes to solving business problems (some of course will have plenty of axes to grind when it comes to their own positions and research, but that is quite another matter). You should be able to rely on faculty members for judicious, impartial, informed opinions.

We will discuss the role of faculty in a little more detail in Chapters 3 and 7.

Are professors people too?

Yes, of course they are. Most of those I have met over the years have been friendly and approachable. Most enjoy teaching, and most like working with students. Most have no illusions about their roles; they are not gurus passing on wisdom to acolytes, they are professionals engaged in a working partnership with other professionals. And too, most are aware that they are providing a service which the students are paying for. They should be treated as mentors and colleagues, not ivory tower geniuses.

There are exceptions to this rule, of course, and any student unfortunate enough to run into them will have to make some choices as to how to deal with the situation. If the situation does arise, talk it over with peers and other business school staff, and try to arrive at a sensible solution.

Other students

These are an often overlooked resource, but in fact, fellow students can be a very valuable resource. Consider that in an MBA class of, say, 120 people, there will be a very broad mix in terms of socio-economic background, education, business experience and technical/functional skills. In many of the more international schools, there will also be a broad socio-cultural mix. All this means is that each student in this group has around him or her 119 other individuals with different experiences, knowledge and approaches to problems and issues. Tapping into their knowledge and ideas can be a valuable source of inspiration. We shall have more to say on this subject in Chapter 5 when we come to discuss working in teams. For the moment, though, you should consider your fellow students as part of the resource mix.

Yourself

As we mentioned above, the student himself or herself has an important input into the educational process; but it is also useful to see yourself as part of the resource package, part of the elements that go to make up the MBA experience. What you bring to that experience is a package which includes your own brain/memory/cognitive abilities, your background, your education, your experience and your ideas. In classroom discussions, in project and work groups and in social situations, you will be making an important input, which will affect not only your own experience but those of your colleagues on the programme.

Another aspect, not to be overlooked, is personal physical capabilities. The MBA is a long and sometimes gruelling programme which will take its toll of the student, both mentally and physically. Fatigue can result in as many bad decisions or mistakes as ignorance or miscalculation. (As we suggest in Chapter 2, one ideal preliminary to any MBA programme is a good holiday.) It is important to know your own physical limitations, how far you can push yourself before burnout sets in; and when it does, how to recuperate quickly and get back into the game.

What is this 'MBA experience'?

It sounds like a day out at a theme park, doesn't it? But as a term, I think it works (I didn't invent it, by the way). There is so much more to the MBA than just courses and case studies. There is project work, team working with other students, networking with students, faculty and potential employers, and there is the social life, itself an important element in bonding and building networks. The MBA is more than just an episode in one's education. It really is an 'experience'.

Developing a knowledge management strategy

Knowledge management as a discipline is so much in its infancy and so little is known about it that it may seem unfair to suggest that MBA students need to develop their own knowledge management strategies during the programme; surely that is one of the skills they come to learn, not something they must bring to the table?

I disagree. First of all, knowledge management is something we all *do*, and what the present-day thinkers in knowledge management are trying to do is understand and conceptualize a process which we mostly take for granted. Second, I believe you have to start making knowledge work for you, right from Day One of the MBA experience.

It is first of all important to understand what we mean by 'knowledge'. A surprising number of management books continue to make no distinction between 'knowledge' and 'information'. Others do but get the definitions wrong, like assuming that knowledge is something you make yourself while information is something others transmit to you. Wrong; knowledge *can* be transmitted from other sources, and it is the acquisition of knowledge, rather than mere assemblages of fact, which marks out true learning. Milan Zelany, who has written widely on this subject, offers a distinction between four grades – data, information, knowledge and wisdom – and his schema is reproduced in Table 1.1 below.

This distinction is discussed in more detail in Chapter 8. Leaving aside the other three, let us concentrate on how knowledge is managed. Here is a simple model which should prove helpful. In it, knowledge management is divided into three classes of activity:

- knowledge acquisition and creation
- knowledge organization and structure
- knowledge use

Knowledge acquisition and creation refers to the activities we commonly associate with learning. Knowledge is either acquired from external sources – books, articles, databases, conversations with experts, and so on – or it is created by applying one's own mind to a body of information and data. When you sit down to work on a case, either alone or with a team, analysing the information presented and working out a solution, you are creating knowledge.

Knowledge organization and structure refers to the management of knowledge once it is acquired/created and prior to its use. Most commonly, knowledge is stored in some way, in software programmes or databases, in paper files or in that most powerful and fragile instrument of all, the human brain. The key task in knowledge organization is to ensure that previously learned or created knowledge can be accessed quickly and efficiently. An

Table 1.1 Taxonomy of Knowledge

	Technology	Analogy (Baking Bread)	Effect	Purpose (Metaphor)
Data	EDP	*Elements*: H_2O, yeast bacteria, starch molecules	Muddling through	Know-nothing
Information	MIS	*Ingredients*: flour, water, sugar, spices + recipe	Efficiency	Know-how
Knowledge	DSS, ES, AI	Coordination of the baking process – result, product	Effectiveness	Know-what
Wisdom	WS, MSS	Why bread? Why this way?	Explicability	Know-why

EDP	=	Electronic Data Processing
MIS	=	Management Information Systems
DSS	=	Decision Support Systems
ES	=	Expert Systems
AI	=	Artificial Intelligence
WS	=	Wisdom Systems
MSS	=	Management Support Systems

Source: M. Zeleny, 'Knowledge vs. Information', in M. Zeleny (ed.), *The Handbook of Information Technology in Business*, London: Thomson Learning, 1999, p. 164.

example for MBA students would be setting up a filing system for notes, reports and other sources of knowledge which they have acquired.

Knowledge use represents the employment of knowledge for some purpose. I take a behavioural theory of knowledge, and have elsewhere defined knowledge as 'the stored potential for action'. All this means is that knowledge exists to serve some purpose (even if we do not necessarily know what that purpose is when we first acquire it). During the course of the first stage of an MBA programme, students usually concentrate on acquiring and storing knowledge, but later, in project work for example, the emphasis switches to using knowledge, to putting previously learned lessons into effect.

Setting up a knowledge management strategy requires attention to all three of these issues. It is tempting to assume that the programme is about acquiring knowledge, first, last and only. It is probably possible to get through an MBA programme by concentrating on this issue, but in order to *maximize value* (that phrase again), knowledge needs to be effectively structured and then it has to be used. Most MBA programmes are quite deliberately set up so that at various stages, especially in project work, the knowledge that students have previously acquired must be used.

And too, do not forget the knowledge you have already acquired which you bring into the programme. No MBA student is a *tabula rasa*, though as we will discuss in the next chapter, one of the first and most important tasks is to get rid of previous preconceptions. But preconceptions are not knowledge (they might almost be its antithesis). To repeat, every student who comes to the MBA programme brings with them a working bank of knowledge. One final task for the knowledge management strategy is to incorporate previous learning into the new learning brought about by the programme.

Developing a knowledge management strategy, then, proceeds along the following lines.

1   Assess personal and career goals and the nature of the programme. Get a picture (this will be fuzzy at first, but will clarify over time) of the kinds of knowledge that are required by the programme and that will assist you in reaching your goals.
2   Learn the sources of this knowledge. Find out what knowledge can be accessed from outside sources and where, and what knowledge you will need to create yourself.
3   Develop systems for managing knowledge once it is acquired, whether on computer, on hard copy or in your own

memory. When working on projects or solving problems, use all the resources you have acquired.

4   Assess knowledge in terms of potential use, and be alert to new uses. Be flexible when considering what knowledge might be 'relevant' to a particular problem or issue.

The above is to some extent vague, and because knowledge tends to be highly personal it is accepted that every individual will have his or her own private 'best way' of managing knowledge and solving problems. How the knowledge management strategy works in practice will be dealt with both explicitly and implicitly in the chapters that follow.

Conclusions

The MBA is an experience. More than that, it is *your* experience. You help to make it, and you help to control it. Realizing this brings an awareness of both power and responsibility. Every student has the power to make this experience work for them, to maximize value and drive forward towards personal and career goals. But there is also a responsibility. In order to maximize value, everyone has to take control of their own learning process and take responsibility for their own learning.

I do not mean by this that MBA students should be entirely self-centred. Indeed, this would be impossible. Each MBA class is a community, and its members depend on one another just as do the members of any other organization. A further responsibility, then, is to colleagues, to ensure that one's learning does not happen at the expense of others. If one member of a group is not learning, then it is possible that the learning of others will be hindered.

Chapter 2

Doing the groundwork
Getting started on the MBA

If a man will begin with certainties, he shall end with doubts; but if he will be content to begin with doubts, he shall end with certainties.
Sir Francis Bacon

This chapter looks at the very first stage of the MBA experience, joining the programme. The focus here is on setting up and establishing the kind of system we discussed in the previous chapter.

Most of this chapter is simple common sense. But it is important to approach the MBA methodically and with some pre-planning. Getting the right systems in place before and during the first week or so of the programme can make a big difference, and can reduce the pressure and make learning easier during the later stages.

This chapter then looks at some of the essential aspects of getting started on an MBA programme, including:

- pre-programme preparation
- induction
- learning the ropes
- meeting colleagues
- forming work/study groups
- assessing resources
- setting up systems
- tuning your mind

Pre-programme preparation

As mentioned in the introduction, this book is not about how to choose an MBA, and we are assuming that the reader has already chosen, applied to and been accepted by the business school of their choice. There is usually a gap of some months between the final acceptance and the start of the programme, and during this period there is usually quite a lot to do in terms of putting one's house in order. For full-timers, who are giving up their jobs, there will be a lot of loose ends to tie up at work; it is quite likely that a physical move will be required, possibly even to another country, with consequent problems to solve concerning accommodation and so on. For married MBAs, especially ones with families, there can be further issues concerning spouse/partner's career, schools and the like. All these need to be thought about well in advance and solutions worked out; don't assume these can be dealt with on arrival for the first week of classes.

Part-time MBA students, those on executive programmes and on distance learning programmes, for example, may have different issues to address. Here the key task is to ensure that the study required for the MBA can be fitted into both professional and personal life. If this has not been done already, get a copy of the programme schedule, with dates and times for modules and classes, deadlines for projects and so on, and go through this with colleagues and managers at work and spouse/partner at home. Look out for any likely conflicts and try to resolve them in advance. If insuperable difficulties arise, try contacting the MBA programme office or relevant faculty to see if they can help; don't suffer in silence.

It is also important to be prepared, mentally and physically. To repeat, the MBA will be a long haul, ten months to two years for full-time students depending on the programme they have chosen, and perhaps even longer for students on part-time and executive programmes (and just because the latter are not so concentrated does not mean they are any less gruelling). Try to clear big assignments and projects out of the way a few weeks before the start of the programme. If possible, take a couple of weeks holiday. Be rested, refreshed and alert.

And do not under any circumstances do what one acquaintance of mine did: start a major home refurbishment project two days before the start of the programme!

Induction

Most business schools will offer some sort of induction programme for incoming students. On full-time programmes this can be several days of sessions allowing them to become familiar with the school, its staff and resources and so on. Often these sessions are arranged a few days before the official start of the programme. If such sessions are on offer, do not miss them; they offer a number of benefits including:

- a crash course in knowing what resources the school has to offer and where they can be found
- a chance to meet for the first time your colleagues and some of the school's staff and faculty, and form some first impressions

Part-time students often have to make do with rather less, sometimes only a single session, while distance learning students usually make out worst of all, with an induction manual, video or CD-ROM all that is on offer. These are usually excellent providers of factual information about programmes, information resources and so on, but they miss the second vital element, human contact with colleagues and faculty. This is more generally a problem inherent in distance learning programmes, one which nearly all distance learning providers are aware of and do their best to meet. One popular mechanism is to establish 'support groups' for students in local areas, and encourage them to meet, with or without a faculty member, to discuss problems and work in groups. Most, like the Open University, have a system of tutors scattered throughout the regions where students live, so physical contact with faculty is always possible.

Whatever the programme or the circumstances, use whatever induction sessions or material are available, to the fullest extent. If there is information you feel is lacking, ask questions early. Don't be tempted to skip over this part of the programme on the basis that you can 'pick it up as you go along'. You can, but it will usually cost you in terms of time and attention which could be better spent on other activities.

Learning the ropes

The first few days both before and after the start of the programme are usually spent learning the ropes. This includes

- learning factual information, like the location of the library/information centre, its opening hours and so on;
- getting to know key people, such as the faculty who are teaching the first courses you will take, where their offices are and what their e-mail address are;
- setting up systems, like getting any tickets or passes required for the library/information centre, establishing e-mail accounts and so on;
- generally getting a feel of the ethos or atmosphere of the programme.

Not neglecting the first three points is, again, simple common sense. The latter you may already have begun to do, based on information provided to you by the business school, visits to the school during the application process, previous encounters with students and faculty and so on. Every business school has its own particular atmosphere. This atmosphere comes in part from the location and nature of the physical facilities, and partly from the people, staff, faculty and students, who inhabit the place and make it come alive. Look at things like classrooms and meeting rooms before you start to use them. Look at any canteens, cafes, bars or pubs that may be on campus, and see who uses them. (Find out if the food is any good and how far afield you will have to go to get something you like.)

Some schools' induction programmes including a mentoring process whereby, say, a student in the second year of the programme or further along in the programme more generally mentors an incoming student and helps them get started. This can be really valuable, and your mentor can help in ways that go far beyond the provision of simple factual information. Most mentors are keen to help, but remember they have their own work to be getting on with as well; be friendly and pump them for information (it's what they are there for), but don't overdo it.

Nourishing the inner MBA

The point about food is actually a serious one. There are some people who can survive on an endless diet of black coffee and strong cigarettes, but most of us need something a little more balanced and substantial. A poor diet can lead to low blood sugar levels, which in turn can lead to early fatigue and lack of concentration. Ensuring good health and a proper diet is important. How good the food is at a particular business school is a matter of complete chance (from the student's point of view). One of the best student meals I have ever eaten was at the China-Europe International Business School in Shanghai, while one of the worst was at a business school which is regularly rated in the world's top ten. If your business school is towards the latter end of the continuum, don't just suffer; make alternative arrangements.

If there is no mentor, which is the case in most single-year programmes, then you will in effect have to mentor yourself. Before the programme starts, draw up a list of things you think you will need to know. Concentrate on the main issues which are involved in knowledge management, which were described in the previous chapter. Some of the immediate practical applications of this are discussed below.

Work/study groups

Some MBA programmes like to establish work teams or study groups very early on in the process. Even if the programme as a whole does not establish such groups, individual courses often will. Students may find themselves members of several such groups, depending on the programme and courses. Sometimes people are assigned to a group, others leave students to sort themselves out.

Chapter 5, 'Working in Teams', goes into more detail on the dynamics of such groups. In the initial stages of the programme, the main thing is to get to know your work group members and try to assess their capabilities. Suggest meeting socially: nothing fancy is required, a cup of coffee or a drink will do. Get the group involved in general conversation, not necessarily about the programme, and observe each member, listen to their opinions and watch their reactions. (They will be doing this to you, too.) Build up a mental picture of each of your colleagues, their strengths and their sensitivities, before you begin working together.

Meeting colleagues

Beyond the narrower confines of the work team or study group, there is the broader group of colleagues on the MBA programme. Take advantage of opportunities to mingle and meet. Find out what you can about their backgrounds, and begin the process of building networks and relationships (see Chapter 10 for more on this).

Most business schools have a number of social clubs and groups, and in the first week of the programme, e-mails and notices on bulletin boards begin to advertise their presence. Consider joining some of these (don't spread yourself too thin), and go along to some of their initial meetings to see if you like the atmosphere and the people. If there is no club or society which fits with your interests, consider starting one. As discussed again in Chapter 10, these societies and clubs have two useful purposes:

- they offer good opportunities to meet people and build networks
- they offer even better opportunities to relax and unwind

For reasons discussed in the previous chapter, your colleagues are important to you. You will be working closely with some of them, in study groups and on projects. You will be interacting with them in the classroom, and they will probably play a large part in your social life. Get to know them, and assess their capabilities. Learn strengths, sensitives and susceptibilities. Get the networking process going; be low key at first, as it will take time to get to know people well, but start establishing links. These are people whom you will rely on, certainly on the programme, possibly in your later career as well.

It may sound cold-blooded to treat people as a resource in quite this way. Indeed, if you see people *only* as a resource, then quite possibly you are being cold-blooded. But there is nothing inherently wrong with assessing people on the basis of their own attributes – interests, capabilities, personality and so on – and making an inventory of those attributes for later use, so long as you respect the dignity and humanity of the people with whom you are dealing. Remember to respect everyone you meet. Remember too that they are probably assessing you at the same time, and anti-social behaviour on your part will probably be entered into the database.

The key thing at this stage is, *don't try too hard*. Relax. Have fun. Get to know people and enjoy them for themselves, but watch, listen and remember. The rest will follow naturally.

Assessing resources

In Chapter 1 we offered a resource-based model of the MBA. As soon as possible in the programme, it is a good idea to do an inventory of the available resources. This need not take long, and is probably best done informally. But you should be aware of the nature and location of the following:

- the library/information centre, where it is, its opening hours and conditions of access, and what facilities it offers;
- the names of the faculty who will be teaching you in the first instance, where they are located, their office hours and their e-mail addresses;
- which fellow students you will be working most closely with in the first instance (see above), and their contact addresses;
- your own capabilities, including any strengths or weaknesses you feel you have, any specialist knowledge you can bring to the table and discussions, and, of course, another look at your personal and career goals so that these are kept firmly in sight.

Some of these points will need to be repeated at intervals in the programme, for example, should you change or move on to new study groups or project teams, or when you finish one course or module and move on to another.

ISN'T IT TIME YOU GOT
DOWN TO BUSINESS ?

For students on part-time or Executive MBAs and distance learning MBAs, the same points need to be assessed, but the issue of remote access needs to be factored in. Getting e-mail contacts for all the relevant people is of first-water importance. Usually the programme office will provide these, but if any are missing, now is the time to track them down. Remote access to information sources is also something to be considered. As well as the sources your business school recommends, it is probably worth spending an evening, or several, surfing the Web and looking for sites with information relevant to the courses you are taking in the first instance. Again, this process should be repeated when you finish one course or module and move on to another.

Setting up

It is impossible to overemphasize the importance of getting physically set up and ready to work before you begin doing so. Make sure you have a study or work space set aside at home, with a computer of adequate standard and good IT connections. Do not skimp on these; the computer may become the most important thing in your life over the course of the programme (if your 'significant other' begins showing signs of jealousy, you know you are working too hard). Set up mailing lists or other e-mail management tools you are likely to need, and make sure that any required software has been tested and is running smoothly.

Also recommended is a filing system for hard copy material. The paperless office may be just around the corner (where it has remained firmly throughout most of my lifetime), but today's MBA programmes generate a veritable blizzard of paper. Some of it is actually important, possibly even essential. Make sure you can find it when you need to.

Full-time students will probably find that they are dividing much of their work between home and the business school's campus. Identifying useful working spaces there should also be a priority.

There may be many other requirements as well, but the important thing is to be sure that the tools and resources needed for learning – for knowledge management – are in place before settling down to work. Do not neglect the trivial. Losing an hour trekking down to the nearest office supplies centre to buy computer disks (or a day getting them sent through the post) eats up time which will be at a premium later. If you were ever a Boy Scout in your younger days, you will know the motto: 'Be Prepared'.

Tuning your mind

Possibly the biggest adjustment of all which is required at the outset of an MBA programme is tuning in to a new way of thinking. MBA programmes often offer benefits like 'global vision' and 'broader thinking' or a 'broad experience', but these things do not come automatically. They have to be worked for.

An MBA dean of my acquaintance told me that the first thing incoming students at his school had to do was 'unlearn in order to learn'. Students had to lose some of their previous preconceptions, and open their minds to new ideas and to new ways of analysing and thinking. A good MBA programme will in itself offer many challenges to preconceived ideas, but getting shed of these yourself before beginning the programme will reduce the level of friction as you go along.

The *benefit maximization* process we referred to Chapter 1 depends absolutely on an open mind. Any other option risks rejecting knowledge which might be beneficial, even vital, to success on the programme or later in life. And the other key element of that chapter, the *knowledge management* system, also depends on being as receptive as possible to new ideas, and not ruling any idea out of court just because it seems to conflict with some other idea or ideas. Part of the analysis process contained within knowledge management is the sifting of information and ideas from many different sources, combining them so as to build up as complete and accurate a picture as possible of any given situation. This is not just a tool for managing the MBA experience; it is an everyday part of managerial life.

The importance of an open mind

Norman Dixon, in his classic book *The Psychology of Military Incompetence* (London: Pimlico, 1976) cites the lack of an open mind – the lack of ability to comprehend or act on information which conflicts with preconceived views – as one of the key factors in poor decision making. He cites the example of Field Marshal Montgomery and his staff before the Battle of Arnhem in 1944. Intelligence reports had suggested that there were few German troops in the area around Arnhem, where the Allies planned to drop a division of British paratroopers. When, at a later stage, reports indicated that there were in fact elements of two tank divisions in and around Arnhem, Monty and his staff refused to believe the reports *because the latter conflicted with the staff's own assessment of the situation*. The division was dropped, and the better part of 10,000 British soldiers were killed, wounded or captured.

The relevance of this sort of thinking to business and management is so obvious that it does not really need stating. But it seems a golden rule, in management as elsewhere, that behind every disaster there is a person, or a team, who refused to listen.

How does one then 'open the mind'? Actually, I prefer 'tuning the mind', because I think that is a more accurate picture of what really happens. The process is not just about getting rid of preconceptions, but of sharpening mental processes, becoming better at analysing, looking at issues like risk and security in a new light, and taking an interest in a broad range of subjects and issues whether or not they appear to directly affect one's own situation.

The MBA programme will almost certainly develop these attributes and more. (Also, many MBA programmes select on the basis, at least in part, of potential students' abilities and capabilities in these areas.) But again, it is useful to be as prepared as possible before embarking on the programme. The MBA will have its own traps in terms of knowledge management. It is easy for full-time students to become so engrossed in the mechanics of course work that they forget the big picture, even though most courses and programmes are designed specifically to avoid this. It is easy too for the Executive MBA or distance learner to put the demands of everyday work and home routine first and relegate the MBA to a 'spare time' activity; by then, there is time only to concentrate on the basics of the course, and again the broader picture gets lost.

How to avoid this? A few students try yoga or Zen meditation, or other consciousness-focusing techniques. But in my view, the best way is to opt for a balanced life, with a deliberate emphasis on taking an interest in subjects outside one's ordinary experience. Stay physically healthy and mentally alert. Ensure your schedule has time built in for socializing, with or without colleagues (but preferably at least some of the former). Take advantages of any opportunities the MBA offers to broaden your experience and thinking.

One of the best opportunities for this is the exchange programme which most business schools now offer, and this will be discussed in Chapter 11. But the easiest and best way to broaden your mind is to select as far as possible a range of courses on the programme that will challenge your thinking and stretch your imagination. Courses, their components and how to take them are discussed in the chapter after this one.

Conclusions

As stated at the outset, most of this chapter is common sense. Indeed, as Thomas Reid, the founder of the Common Sense school of philosophy in Scotland in the eighteenth century, once wrote, most problems in life can be solved with the appropriate application of common sense. (Reid did not add, though he makes it implicit in much of his writing, that many of the world's problems are in fact due to a severe shortage of that very commodity.)

The main point of this chapter is to serve as a reminder that there is no substitute for planning and thinking ahead. Learn the ropes, know the nature and location of the resources needed, and be physically and above all mentally fit for the experience that is about to come.

Although the MBA experience has many different aspects, most MBA programmes are built around a formal structure of coursework. The next chapter discusses courses and how they work, while the ones that follow look at various aspects of course work such as case studies, team working and communication.

Chapter 3

Courses
The first channel of knowledge acquisition

Lessons are not given – they are taken.
Cesar Pavese

Most of us can (and probably always will) remember with painful clarity the courses we took as undergraduates. Lecture halls and classrooms that were always too hot or too cold...lecturer at the front droning on, making indecipherable marks on a chalkboard...class sitting in rows facing...trying not to fall asleep...taking down notes which one couldn't read when it came time to revise for exams...focusing on just one aim, absorbing enough knowledge to get a decent mark at the end of term.

It is certainly possible to approach business school courses in the same way, and in particular to concentrate on just one aspect, the final mark or grade. But there is another, rather better way to approach courses, one which will serve to greatly increase the benefits received. This involves looking at courses as *channels of knowledge acquisition*. If business schools can be seen as collections of knowledge resources, as we discussed in Chapter 1, then courses are the first and sometimes the most important means through which students learn and acquire this knowledge. This chapter focuses on defining courses in this way, and on ways of maximizing the knowledge and therefore the value each course provides.

There is so much variety in business school courses in terms of type, subject matter and delivery system that at first glance it might seem difficult to generalize about them. However, there is one obvious and important feature which courses have in common, and that is the point made in the previous paragraph: all are channels by which knowledge is acquired. As the backbone structure of the MBA programme, they define and shape the learning experience. It follows, then, that what courses a student takes will have a very considerable impact on the nature of that experience.

This may seem simple, or at least simplistic. But there are several key points which are not so obvious, and which need reinforcing:

- in order to maximize value, courses should be selected which fit in with the student's personal and career goals, and
- in order to manage knowledge efficiently, it is a good idea to understand some of the philosophy and thinking behind this kind of knowledge channel.

We will deal with both these points in detail later in the chapter. Note that Chapters 4–7 which follow deal in more detail with certain aspects of courses.

Definition

One of the dictionary definitions of a 'course' generally is 'onward movement or intended direction'. This should be born in mind when considering business school courses. They are not random assemblages of knowledge, nor are they (by any means) vessels containing the total sum of knowledge on any subject. Any well-designed course has a purpose and a theme, and generally starts from an introductory position, moves through a gradual unveiling of its theme, and at the end invites conclusions.

Courses thus tend to be didactic in nature. Their theme is set, sometimes seemingly arbitrarily, by the faculty and programme managers who design them. The input of these individuals is usually crucial in determining course design. Especially at advanced levels, no two courses will be the same, even if they are covering what is broadly the same subject.

This is not a bad thing, though there is one important proviso which we will come back to in a moment. Learning, and especially learning about business and management, should not be standardized. There are no simple, rote solutions to managing business and organizations in complex environments such as exist today. Diversity in approach represents one way of mastering rich and complex subjects. The proviso is simply this: to be any good, a course has to recognize that it cannot provide complete and total knowledge of its subject. What a course should aim to do instead is position itself as a framework or skeleton, outlining the *shape* and *nature* of the subject, and giving students a basis from which to advance to further knowledge.

Most courses do three things:

- they provide some fundamental knowledge about the subject;
- they broaden the mind, by posing questions students might not have thought of and encouraging them to seek out and develop answers;
- they provide a framework for further knowledge, which can be derived either through further study (formal or undertaken by oneself) or personal experience, and which can be learned during the course or long after.

The Marketing 1 course you take in first term cannot possibly tell you everything you need to know about marketing. What it will (or should) do, though, is start to explain the basics of what marketing is about. In doing so, it challenges your preconceptions of what marketing is, and encourages you to redefine the subject. It provokes questions which stimulate you to do things such as undertake further reading so as to add to your stock of knowledge, take elective courses in marketing later in the programme to help define particular areas of interest, and finally, in your career after the programme, to have an understanding of and sympathy with marketing issues even if your work does not directly involve you in marketing. A really good course is one where, five years later, you receive a piece of information and are able to make sense of it (convert it into knowledge) because of what you remember from the course.

The debate about courses

Education has its fashions and trends like everything else, and in the 1980s the idea of business school 'courses' *per se* came under attack. The prevailing model whereby a faculty member lectured to the class was attacked as being 'chalk and talk', lacking in practical experience or application. The idea of lecturers imparting knowledge to students was seen as 'elitist'. Finally, the classroom was seen as being an artificial world, divorced from real business situations.

There was some truth in all these accusations, and most business schools responded by changing their pedagogical methods, with the result that most are rather better at teaching than they were two or three decades ago. But the basic course structure of MBA programmes worldwide has largely survived, basically because no one has been able to come up with any substitute for them. Practical experience is wonderful and there is no substitute for it (see Chapter 9), but it is now generally recognized that practical experience requires context and background, and that can be learned in the classroom just as well as anywhere else.

Lecturers and professors are no longer remote, godlike figures (okay, some of them think they are, and it is probably best not to disillusion them), but they *are* specialists and they do have unique levels of knowledge. I argue that one should not learn *from* faculty so much as learn *through* them. See more on the role of faculty below.

Types of courses

As most readers will probably be aware from reading their programme syllabus, courses fall into two, or sometimes three, different types. Although various names are used, I am sticking here with the most common: *core courses*, *integrative courses* and *elective courses*.

Core courses are offered in the first term(s) of the programme. They are usually based on specific functions (marketing, finance, accounting, etc.) or on specific areas of background knowledge such as business economics. They are nearly always mandatory for all students. (Some schools make a distinction between functional and background courses, but in practice both usually have the features of core courses.)

Core courses are often the Cinderellas of the MBA programme. Students (and faculty) are usually much more interested in electives, which are considered to be more exciting and fun to take (and teach). But do not neglect the core courses. They have their name for a reason: they are the basic building blocks on which all further knowledge about management must rest: the fundamentals without which it is not possible to proceed much further. One of the finest features of the MBA is the all-round nature of the knowledge and experience it offers, and how it meshes different areas of knowledge together; but to get to this stage, you have to have the core knowledge in the first place.

Elective courses, as the name implies, are chosen by students themselves, and usually come in the final year or terms of the programme. Many business schools pride themselves on the range and choice of elective courses they can offer. Electives are popular because (1) they are chosen by the individual (let's face it, it is always more fun to do something you have chosen to do rather than something that is assigned for you) but more importantly (2) because they allow students to tailor their MBA experience by either specializing in a particular field or acquiring a broader range of background knowledge, or both.

When choosing elective courses, don't just pick the ones that look like 'fun'. Keep personal and career goals firmly in mind. Use the selection of electives to maximize the knowledge you acquire from the MBA programme. Focus on your chosen special area (if you have one) by all means, but try also to take courses that will broaden the mind and open up new horizons. If possible, think about taking one or two electives well outside your chosen area. Marketing specialists might consider doing a couple of courses that focus on technology management, or on number-crunching disciplines such as quantitative analysis. Those heading for a career in corporate finance might consider electives in communications or cross-cultural management as possibly adding important new dimensions to their skills, and so on. Using electives in this way gives the student a way of tailoring his or her own skills profile, and this should both score points with recruiters *and* be of valuable benefit in one's own work and career.

The third category, *integrative courses*, is something of a mixed bag. Different business schools have different definitions and sometimes use different names. Integrative courses tend to be cross-functional in nature, focusing on issues such as strategy, interpersonal skills and so on. They contain necessary knowledge, and as such are usually mandatory, but they do not fit neatly into the boxes of functions or background knowledge. These courses are among the hardest to design and deliver, but they can be very rewarding. Often 'fuzzy' in nature, they home in on some of the real-life problems and dilemmas which managers must face.

The entrepreneurship ghetto

One of the things I find most perplexing about business schools today is how they continue to define 'entrepreneurship' as a special subject area – usually for elective courses only – and focus it towards students who are interested in doing start-ups. There seems to be a notion that starting a small business is 'entrepreneurial' and that, by definition, anything else is not.

Leaving aside the fact that many successful small business owners, including some quite rich ones, are most definitely not 'entrepreneurs', there should really be no such thing as 'non-entrepreneurial business'. Gurus like Tom Peters have been clamouring for years for large firms to become *more* entrepreneurial in their outlook. In the post-industrial economy which we are now entering, an entrepreneurial approach is a distinct advantage in any walk of business life.

Entrepreneurship is not a discipline, it is a way of thinking. Entrepreneurship is demonstrated by assessing situations, analysing risks, seeking out opportunities and maximizing value from them. It is not so different in essence from the benefit maximization approach I have been urging students to take to their MBAs. By looking for opportunities to grow your own knowledge, you are in effect being entrepreurial; the same mindset can stand you in good stead later when you come to grow your profits, no matter what size or structure of firm you are working for.

Delivery methods

There are many methods for delivering knowledge through the structure of a course. Just some of them include conventional classroom lectures, case studies (see Chapter 4), written projects (see Chapter 6) classroom discussions (see Chapter 7), videos, computer-assisted learning packages, simulations and micro-worlds. Many business schools and faculty members prefer a mix of different methods, as the different and often interactive delivery systems provide more mental stimulation for students. Each method requires different responses and analysis, thus providing the potential for a broader look at the subject and a greater depth of learning.

In practice, the variety of delivery systems is limited only by available technical resources and the imaginations of the lecturers and programme designers. In the 1990s, a colleague and I ran an elective course at London Business School where, in one project, we asked students to take the part of different parties engaged in renegotiating a complex contract. (We apportioned marks in part according to who came out of the deal well, but in part also on whether the deal looked 'genuine' and likely to last.) There was obvious benefit from the exercise, but the novelty of it also stimulated students and drew more imagination and crea-tivity from them in response.

Distance learning

Students engaged in distance learning are likely to have a slightly narrower mix of systems than those in full-time or Executive programmes. There is more reliance here on written material, videos and, increasingly, computer-assisted learning programmes delivered over the Internet. These last in partic-ular are often very sophisticated, as are many of the video cases now available. My only comment here is that, excellent though these are, they miss some of the subtlety that incurs when learning from others face to face. Try to compensate for this lack by engaging in discussion groups, regular meetings with tutors and so on.

Aims and processes

Most courses proceed through a fairly simple set of stages. They begin by offering foundational knowledge, build on that with more complex terms and ideas which lead the students to analyse and in some cases challenge what they have learned, and finally draw conclusions about what is/can be known about the subject. All are thus didactic to some extent, although there are variations on this theme: the Canadian management guru Henry Mintzberg once wrote that he preferred to simply place information/knowledge before students and let them analyse it and draw their own conclusions, but most others prefer a more active relationship between faculty and student, with the students eventually being shown a picture of some aspect of management as the faculty has conceived it.

This last point is quite important. A course does not represent 'truth' about its particular aspect of management, it represents its designer and presenter's idea of what 'truth' is (perhaps the two are practically indistinguishable, but the possibility that they are not should always be borne in mind). As such, no course is a perfect picture; it is – or should be – as we said above, a framework rather than a snapshot.

A second point, related to the first, is that the MBA course has not yet been designed (though a few have tried) which encompasses *all* of management. Holism is found in the full complement of courses, not any one course itself. Courses relate to one another, in the same way that the functional disciplines of management relate to one another or a company relates to its customers, employees, and so on. There is always a whole that is bigger than the sum of the parts. Look for linkages between courses as you go along. Sometimes they will be pointed out to you, others you will have to find for yourself.

The role of faculty

Hitherto we have discussed faculty as a resource, as the repositories of certain kinds of specialist knowledge and as designers and deliverers of courses. The usual way of looking at the relationship between students and faculty is a straightforward dyad.

As the figure below shows, however, there is another approach, one which requires viewing faculty as guides or signposts towards further information. Faculty don't know everything about their subject, and hardly any claim to do so. Nearly all, however, have a pretty shrewd idea of where to go to find more

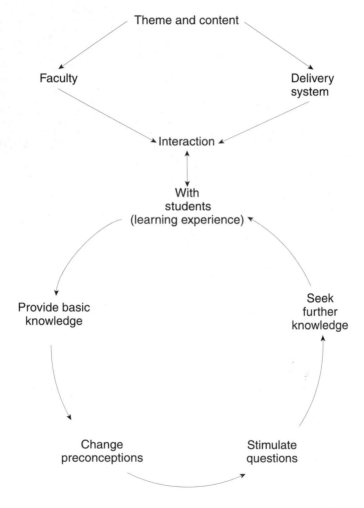

Figure 3.1 How business school courses work

NATURALLY THIS ISN'T AS STRAIGHTFORWARD
AS IT LOOKS . . . .

knowledge. They can direct the student to written or on-line sources, suggest colleagues who may have more knowledge, make introductions to people in industry who may have access to further specialist knowledge, help design programmes of inquiry which will allow the student to learn more about the issues that interest him or her, and so on.

Most faculty are happy to be used in this way. Intelligent and interesting inquiries from students are always welcome. Faculty are busy people, with their own career goals, research interests and so on, but they respect intelligence and ability when they see it. My own experience is that it is far more interesting to work with students who are demanding and challenging, interested in seeking further knowledge and developing their own skills, than it is to work with those who sit passively waiting for information to be delivered to them.

Faculty design courses based around subjects and areas of personal interest to them. Their careers and to some extent their egos are involved in the subject matter, and vice versa. Working with students who show a lively interest in their subject and are seeking to expand the boundaries of what the course provides is usually a rewarding experience for them as well for the students. Developing a good working relationship with course faculty should be an important asset in managing knowledge.

Maximizing value from courses

Having described what MBA courses are, how they function and a little of the aims and philosophy behind them, let us now cut to the chase. How can MBA students maximize value through courses?

Courses are not, or should not be, passive experiences where students wait for lecturers to impart knowledge to them. They should be creative, challenging experiences. Like all the rest of the educational experience, this requires input from the student. By choosing courses that will expand thinking and knowledge, by creative input in the classroom, by challenging ideas presented to them, and above all by going beyond the basic framework of the course to seek out new knowledge, students can make each course into an individual learning experience.

Course selection

A primary method for maximizing value is of course course selection. Where options are given or elective courses are offered, choose the courses which will best serve your own ends. This does *not* mean choosing courses where you are already familiar with the material and where you can expect to obtain a high mark. Instead, choose courses which expand existing knowledge, give access to new areas of knowledge, challenge previous views and stretch and broaden your thinking. Consider choosing courses where you have no background or experience at all, the window into a new world can be exhilarating and rewarding, even if the experience is a little frightening at times.

Course work

Chapters 4–7 give more detail on specific aspects of course work, but in general terms, the student should always be looking to do more than is expected of him or her. In business school courses, there is almost never a simple choice of a right answer and a wrong answer to any question (except perhaps in accounting courses). There is, however, usually a simple answer and a more complex one. When analysing cases and scenarios, look beyond the simple facts as presented and try to build up a complete picture. Look for solutions which not only solve the problem first presented but also offer potential for further value to be added to the company or organization to be discussed. In classroom discussions and lectures, don't just listen to the words being spoken, analyse them and think of positive responses – even if you never say them. In work teams and study groups, make positive contributions and encourage others to do the same, so that all end up with the best possible result.

Work outside the framework of the course

By going beyond the framework of the course – that is, the lectures, cases and so on that have been designed and delivered by programme faculty – it is possible to add more value than even the course's designers conceived. What is more, by using the course as a platform to seek out new knowledge, it is possible to tailor even the most basic core course until it becomes an individual learning experience.

How is this done? The process begins by analysing the course material, classroom discussions, lectures, cases and so on, and asking questions. If questions asked in class do not yield desired results, go out and try to answer them yourself. Use the business school's library/information centre for some kinds of searches. Talk to fellow students and especially to faculty, and pick their brains. Find out what they know, ask their opinions, get their views on your ideas and use those views to revise your own thinking. Set yourself questions and then set out to find answers.

This may not be easy, particularly in a fairly high pressure environment like an MBA programme where you may find it takes 10-12 hours a day just to keep up with what is expected of you. Well, here's some news; it isn't going to get any easier. Life in management, especially senior management, is hectic and pressurised (readers on Executive programmes do not need to be told this) and it is quite likely that there will *never* be time enough to ask questions, analyse ideas and pursue knowledge. At least, not if you plan your time in a conventional way. But management is increasingly *about* knowledge, and a manager without knowledge, or with insufficient knowledge, is likely to go the way of the dodo. Your firm's competitive edge and your own career may depend on your ability to get, acquire and use knowledge. Consider this, when prioritizing your time.

Analyse and challenge

Any piece of information delivered during a course should be looked at, analysed and used as appropriate. Never accept anything on trust; look at ideas from different angles and see if they make sense. If they do not, challenge the source. If the source is a faculty member teaching the course or a colleague in class, ask them to explain themselves. If something does not make sense, don't just shrug and accept it. Equally, if new knowledge conflicts with old knowledge, don't throw the new knowledge out if it cannot be reconciled with the old (remember Field Marshal Montgomery at Arnhem). And remember that just because something does not appear relevant at the moment does not mean it will not become so later.

By doing these things, the student should achieve two goals. One is a broader and better quality of knowledge about the subject being taught. The second is the development of an analytical yet questing mindset. The mental skills involved here are exactly those which are increasingly required in a career in management.

Dealing with failure

It does happen that students take courses which, in their view, do *not* deliver the required knowledge and thus are not satisfactory. If it is sensed that this is beginning to happen, then here are some options.

- Analyse your own reaction. What exactly is not working for you? Are you certain it is the course that is at fault, or do you perhaps have preconceptions which are getting in the way?
- Look at how the course is being delivered; it may be the method rather than the content that is the problem. Talk to the course's teaching faculty and see if there is some way in which you can compensate (look for some outside reading, etc.).
- If the content really is failing to live up to expectations, consider developing your own programme of additional learning, again perhaps through outside work. But discuss the problem with course faculty, and see if a resolution can be found.
- If all else fails, most business schools have agreed procedures for student complaints of this nature. This route should only be followed if the processes above have been exhausted.
- *Don't do nothing.* This is your experience, you are paying for it, and it is your problem if the value you expect is not delivered. Whether the problem lies with you, the design of the course or its content, seek an early resolution and get your knowledge management processes back on track.

Courses and the knowledge management process

Courses are initially exercises in knowledge acquisition, but nearly all will expect students to organize and use knowledge as well. (For more on these three stages of the knowledge management process, see Chapter 1.)

Knowledge acquisition is a cognitive process. In the context of an MBA course, students will directly acquire knowledge and information through two basic senses, hearing and sight. The brain manages the signals received through these senses and stores them, in a way that not even brain scientists themselves understand fully, so that we can recall knowledge from our memories. Indirectly, they will also acquire knowledge stored in written or electronic media, such as reports, case studies, books, journal articles, web pages and so on. This flow can be relentless and unceasing, and the knowledge thus acquired will have little value unless systems are in place to organize it.

Indirectly acquired knowledge, referred to above, needs to be organized in files or databases. I myself am very bad at filing, and on occasion this costs me; knowledge previously acquired, sometimes at some pain and cost, vanishes without trace because I can no longer lay hands on the required piece of paper or computer file. Filing seems boring and time-wasting; but in fact, it is at the heart of knowledge management.

Directly acquired knowledge, stored in one's own memory, is a different matter, and again we are confronted with the fact that we know really very little about the workings of the human brain. But one important observed phenomenon is that memory, like a dog, behaves better when exercised. Recalling and using stored knowledge is a way of keeping it fresh. If you play the piano every day, chances are you can play it without much conscious effort; it is a regularly used skill and the brain is familiar with its patterns. If you have not played the piano in ten years, it can be a real effort to remember where middle C is, and you might have to play quite a while before the brain finds the old patterns and brings them back. 'Use it or lose it' would seem to be a good motto for knowledge stored in human memory. (This is quite unlike knowledge stored in computer memory, which is imperishable and lasts forever; or, at least, until IT upgrades your software and accidentally deletes all your database files.)

Knowledge use will inevitably be called for. Case studies and projects require analysis and decisions. Classroom discussions provoke questions which you will have to answer. Again, this is valuable preparation for the 'real world' of management which will follow the programme. Every day, managers are required to use knowledge when assessing situations and risks, seeking opportunities and making decisions. Indeed, can anyone think of any other reason why managers exist? Even the most primitive command-and-control management systems were basically about managers gathering and using knowledge; and in the post-industrial economy, as we have seen, knowledge is an asset and a commodity. It is, quite literally, management's stock in trade.

Conclusions

This chapter has looked at courses, as the first and one of the most important channels of delivering knowledge in an MBA programme. As such, it may fall into the category of 'motherhood statements'. Everyone *knows* courses are important; they are the stuff of which the MBA is made of. What we have tried to do here is offer a new way of thinking about courses, one which stresses:

- their role as frameworks, rather than offerings of complete knowledge
- the opportunities they offer for active learning
- the role played by faculty, and the opportunities for further learning through faculty-student interaction
- how courses fit into the knowledge management process

The final aim has been to suggest that by taking an active and creative approach to course selection and course work, it is possible to add further value to the MBA experience.

Certain elements of course work offer special opportunities for benefit maximization. These include case studies, working in teams or groups with other students, written reports and communications, and classroom discussions. Each of these is discussed in turn in the chapters that follow.

Chapter 4

Case studies
Exercises in management skills

I am not determining a point of law, I am restoring tranquillity.
Edmund Burke

The case study is one of the most common teaching tools encountered by most MBA students. It has a venerable history, being first developed and used at Harvard Business School in the 1920s. Case studies had been used in legal teaching for some time before and the founders of Harvard Business School, looking for tools they could adapt rather than develop from scratch, hit upon the case method as the right way of teaching management.

The idea quickly took off, and some American business schools became infamous for the number of cases they assigned during each term or course. Today, there is somewhat less reliance on case studies, partly because they are seen to have certain drawbacks (see below) and partly because other more sophisticated teaching tools are now available. However, the case study remains important. A well-produced case study remains a good concise way of conveying a lot of information and, at the same time, prompting students to undertake analysis of problems and use their knowledge to come up with solutions. Cases are cheap and cheerful forms of learning, in many ways better adapted to providing core or foundational learning than their more complex successors such as simulations and microworlds.

Cases are also used in some forms of undergraduate teaching, and readers may already be familiar with the basics of the method. Even so, this chapter is probably worth a read. As well as describing the mechanics of case studies, we look at approaches to resolving and presenting cases, and at ways of maximizing the benefits of this kind of work.

This chapter looks at the basics of case studies, and some of the advantages and drawbacks of this teaching method. It then goes on to suggest some steps for reading and analysing a case, resolving the issues described, and presenting this resolution to course faculty or to the class. It discusses three different approaches to case studies in terms of utility and benefit maximization. Finally, we look at the role of cases in the broader context of knowledge management.

Simulations and microworlds

Simulations are in effect 'dynamic cases', where students play through the scenario they have been given, dealing with the consequences of their decisions and with new problems and issues as they arise. Microworlds are more complex still, computer-generated and managed models which can mimic the actions of an entire sector or market. They are widely used in executive training, but are less common for MBA students, in large part because they are so complex that managing them correctly requires a very high level of previous knowledge – the kind of knowledge that the MBA programme in fact aims to provide. Simulations are sometimes used in advanced level courses, however.

I will not describe the use and value of these in any detail, except for a few passing references in this chapter, and will concentrate on case studies. Though they are more complex and containing more knowledge than simple case studies, their management in terms of personal learning is approximately the same. Much of this chapter should also apply to simulations.

Definitions

A case study, then, is a description of a (usually) real-life situation in which a company, team or manager found themselves. Usually there is a problem or crisis of some sort which requires a solution. The case study presents background information about the company, its products, customers, employees, financial situation and so on, and immediate information about the problem needing to be solved. Most end with a question or a 'hook' designed to stimulate a response from the reader, phrased in varying ways but all essentially meaning 'How would you go about solving this problem?' In MBA programmes, students will then be asked to present the answers to this question in either written form, verbal discussion in class, or both.

There is considerable variety in terms of length and style. Harvard Business School cases, which are widely used around the world, tend to be long and formal (betraying their origins in law), and often provide immense quantities of complex financial data. Other scenarios can be less formal, often taking the form of transcripts of conversations, or including copies of correspondence between the principals involved. Long, intricate cases are common, but many faculty also make use of short 'mini-cases' or 'scenarios', often developed by themselves or close colleagues, or derived from textbooks; these may be only a few pages, or even a few paragraphs.

Solving v. resolving

It used to be common to speak of doing case study work as 'solving' cases. This implied that they were a puzzle, to which the 'right' solution could be found. (Again, this is a throwback to the origins of case studies in law.)

I prefer to speak of 'resolving' cases because in most good case studies there is no right or wrong answer. Good cases encourage multidisciplinary approaches and plurality of thinking. In business, unlike law, situations are seldom black or white. In the real world, there is nearly always more than one way to solve a business problem, and good case studies reflect this. The aim, then, should not be to find the 'right' answer (i.e. the one you think is expected), but to find an answer that 'works' and is likely to succeed.

The case study method is used in nearly every discipline taught in business schools, and so there are finance cases, marketing cases, operations management cases and so on. In these instances, it is usually fairly clear that the student(s) are expected to resolve a finance, marketing, ops management, etc. problem. More tricky to deal with are cases which call for a cross-functional approach to their resolution. These describe a general business problem, and leave it up to students to work out what kind of action will be required to resolve it; often a combination of methods and techniques is required.

Advantages and disadvantages of the case study method

Cases are great for foundational learning in particular because they are quick and easy. Short mini-cases or scenarios can be read and digested in a few minutes. Longer Harvard-style cases will take longer, but rarely more than an hour, if that, for a preliminary read through. Though the situations they describe are complex, the learning they provide (once you get to it) is often simple and easy to digest and manage. Particularly if they are taught in an open-ended manner (that is, not focusing on a single 'right' solution), they offer chances to approach the problem from a number of different ways and so add real learning value.

Classroom discussion of cases is a particularly useful learning tool. Offering the same case study at the same time to twenty or thirty MBA students may seem as if teaching faculty are asking for all to give the same answer. In fact, the greater the number of different answers that comes back the better, particularly if most or all seem to 'work' and look like genuine resolutions. Discussing, and arguing over, these apparently competing solutions opens up the possibility of multiple roads to success, showing a wider vision of both problem and resolution.

There are disadvantages to the case study method, and three in particular have come under attack. The first is that case studies are static: they offer a single issue or set of issues which need to be resolved. Students may come up with solutions, but they have no way of knowing whether their idea would have worked. Faculty often conclude discussions of case studies by explaining 'what the company did next', but this does not necessarily

HOW WOULD YOU LIKE TO BE
A CASE STUDY... · · · ?

provide reassurance (unless, of course, your method of resolution was identical to that chosen by the company).

Second, case studies are perforce written about events in the past. Because they are real life studies, by the time the research has been done and the case study written, the events described will inevitably have receded and, so critics say, be less relevant (one academic describes case studies as 'the best way to solve the business problems of twenty years ago'). Against this, though, it should be pointed out that certain fundamental problems and issues in business are pretty well timeless, and so long as cases are kept reasonably up to date and describe common issues, then there is no harm in using them. The point of a case study is not to solve the problems of IBM *per se*, it is to *re*solve the particular set of issues and problems described (which just happen to have occurred at IBM).

Third, nearly all cases describe companies that ultimately succeeded; very few use examples of failure. Despite several decades of observing how Japanese business culture, for example, exploits and learns from failure in a systematic way, most Western business academics have a horror of describing failure. They see using cases of failure as too pessimistic, too downbeat, arguing that one should not teach students how to fail. This ignores the deep learning that can be drawn from case studies of failures and errors.

Despite these caveats, however, the advantages of the case study method remain strong. It is important to recognize the limitations of this method, and it is particularly important not to get too wrapped up in the individual company or people being described. Ultimately, cases are about abstract learning. Look beyond the situation and find the knowledge buried deeper within.

Reading and analysing cases

As mentioned above, most cases can be read fairly quickly and simply. Analysing them for deeper levels of information and knowledge is a longer process.

How a case should be tackled in practice depends to some extent on how one is working. Some case study assignments are on an individual basis, while others assign teams or study groups of students to come up with a joint solution. The other important distinction here is between cases which are presented in text (usually on paper), and those that appear visually on CDs or videos.

No matter what the format, the first step is usually to have a first read through (or watch, if this a video case), preferably on your own. This should be fairly quick, with the emphasis on getting a first look at the bigger picture. What is the firm being described? What business is it in? What are its core products, markets, customers? What is its basic financial position (healthy, unhealthy, teetering on the brink, etc.)? By the time this stage is over, you will have an outline understanding of the problem.

Then go through the case again. This time, look for the details. Pull out any points of information that provide background and/or illuminate the problem. If you are working on paper, underlining or highlighting text can be useful way of identifying these points, so that when referring back to the case you can pull out information points easily, without needing to re-read large chunks of text. With video cases, or if reading a text case on screen, it will be necessary to take notes, but again these can be structured so as to summarize the key points. This is also the stage when you can attempt to find and dispose of any red herrings which the case's writers may thoughtfully have provided for you to stumble across.

By now the reader will be fully familiar with the case. Using the information gathered in the previous stages, build up a detailed picture of what you know about the company, its markets, products, environment, financial situation, employees, the quality of its management and any other information provided, and also the problem the company is facing. If there is time, write down a short summary of all this information in your own words. This is not a wasted step, you can adapt and re-use this material when developing your final presentation.

Next, focus on the problem. Does this appear to be a functional problem, that is, one relating specifically to some business function such as marketing, finance or human resources management? Or is this a strategic issue, concerning not how the company operates but its goals and directions? Or is this a complex issue, requiring a broad-based approach? It is at this

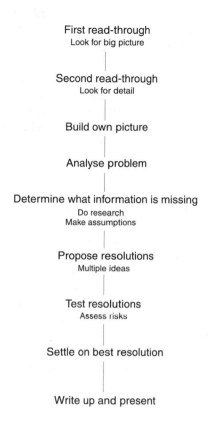

First read-through
Look for big picture

Second read-through
Look for detail

Build own picture

Analyse problem

Determine what information is missing
Do research
Make assumptions

Propose resolutions
Multiple ideas

Test resolutions
Assess risks

Settle on best resolution

Write up and present

Figure 4.1   Steps in case study analysis

point that, if you are working in a team or study group, the group should come together for discussion (group work in earlier stages is possible too, but here it becomes essential). Spend some time over this, and be sure that the problem is fully defined and understood before looking at resolutions.

At this point, if not before, it may seem that some of the information you need to develop resolutions is missing. This may be due to the constraints of the case itself (there was not enough space to fit the information in) or this may be deliberate on the part of the writers (after all, managers in real business situations seldom have complete sets of information either). There are two ways to approach this problem. First, if there is time, supplementary research can be undertaken. If you know the company and the sector, it may be possible to generate additional information from readings, journals, databases or websites. This is particularly useful when building up background information.

The second option is to make assumptions about missing information: that is, effectively 'fill in the blanks' with educated guesswork and then treat that guesswork as if it was part of the scenario. For example, a marketing case may talk about the company's gross sales of a particular product and give current market share, but may not tell you how fast the market is growing. If you feel this is important, and there is not time to research the real figure, arrive at an estimate of what you feel is likely, and then treat that estimate as part of the information set you work from to solve the case. Two cautions, though: first, always check that your assumptions are realistic and reasonable (i.e., run them by someone else who might know better than you), and second, always check that the faculty teaching the course are amenable to this method; some do not like assumptions, and prefer students to work only from verifiable information. Note too that providing reliable assumptions may in itself involve further research.

When all available information has been gathered, now is the time to begin developing resolutions. For groups, there are various possible techniques. Members can be asked to come up with potential resolutions on their own, which are then put forward for discussion. (It is usually a good idea to get all the proposals on the table before beginning to discuss the relative merits of each.) The resolution eventually agreed on will be that which members think is best or, more commonly, a jointly agreed on resolution which combines features of several proposals. Alternatively, the entire process can be thrashed out in the course of a group discussion.

At all costs, avoid the temptation to come up with one resolution and then stick to that. Go through all the information and look at the problem again. Come up with as many different realistic resolutions as possible, then look at them all. Quite often, you will find that several have good features and that it may be possible to combine them.   Don't be afraid to question your previous views of the case. This looks like a marketing problem, but is it really? If the issue concerns product, might not operations and human resource management also be involved? What inputs from those directions could resolve the case?

When a full list of potential resolutions has been compiled, begin testing them. Again, this can be done alone or in the context of a group discussion. There are various ways of testing, but the easiest is probably to ask of each resolution, 'Why wouldn't this work?' If there is information in the case study which suggests a high probability of failure, you may need to junk the idea. If you can see no clear reason why the resolution would not work, put it forward. Ultimately, you should come down to a handful of ideas, of which you or the group can pick and choose which is most appropriate and likely to work.

It may well happen that *none* of the proposed solutions looks likely to work, or that there is a high probability of failure in any case. (Don't worry too much if you do arrive at this point; this is highly realistic.) At this point the assessment of risks needs to take a slightly different turn. Having established various proximate causes of failure, it now remains to be seen whether and how these causes can be guarded against. What steps can be taken to lay off risk? The resolution which allows for the best and most realistic measures in this direction may begin to emerge as your preferred option.

Or will it? You may decide to go for a bolder approach, if the reward seems worth it. In the military, it is always argued that there is a fine line between bravery and insanity (or, more unkindly, stupidity). The same line exists in management, and should not be crossed if possible. Remember that, in real life, you would have to answer to top management and the shareholders for your behaviour (a fact which temporarily escapes the notice of rogue traders, for example).

The resolution on which you or your group ultimately settle is down to yourselves. Ultimately, it will depend in part on your own nature and characters, and so it should. There is still room for individual style in management, and vision and the ability to carry it out will in most cases come good over more rigid, do-it-by-numbers thinking. Be creative in your approach, but do not lose touch with the fundamentals.

The final step is the presentation. Chapters 6 and 7 discuss some of the elements of written and verbal communication. Presentations should always be carefully planned and drafted. Ideally, a case write-up or presentation should include the following:

- a description of the company and its situation (including any assumptions which have been made, clearly defined as such)
- an analysis of the problem or problems the company faces
- a quick discussion of the most important potential resolutions and the problems and risks associated with each
- the resolution ultimately adopted, with reasons why, and a full and frank assessment of the risks and rewards attendant on it

Lengths will vary according to the nature of the case and the preference of teaching faculty, but 2–3 pages is usually a good length to aim at for written presentations; verbal ones should rarely take more than five minutes. Be professional in your approach. Explain your conclusions clearly, and be sure that your reasoning is also clearly explained. Don't try to hide or explain away facts that contradict your reasoning; be frank and realistic about problems and risks. Finally, be clear what result you expect to accrue if your recommendations are implemented.

Approaches to case study resolution

There are, in general terms, three different ways to approach case study resolution. Which approach is chosen will depend in part on the case itself, but I argue that the best method of all is to try a synthesis of all three. This can be tricky to design, and the results can be even more difficult to write up or present, but the value added in terms of additional learning is considerable.

The first and most basic method is the *problem-solving approach*. In this approach, students concentrate on the situation and issues described in the case study. The first and foremost aim is to find a resolution which appears to work and would, if implemented in a real-life situation, offer the company a good chance of success. In terms of learning, the main aim is to learn how problems of a similar type can be resolved; possibly it is felt this information will come in useful in either later cases or after the programme.

Attention to this issue is obviously necessary, if only for practical reasons. The problem *must* be resolved; if it is not, then the company might fail. Faculty and colleagues on the course will want to know what resolution has been reached, and marks or grades may depend on this. On the other hand, attention to this issue alone risks missing out on opportunities for further learning.

The *further learning* approach treats the case study not as a problem in itself, but as an opportunity to learn further and expand knowledge of issues related to the case. For example, a case about human resource management may raise issues concerning training and recruitment. Taking these issues as a starting point, the student might become involved in deeper reading and research on these issues, both in relation to the case and more generally.

Using the questions provoked by case studies in this way can be a very valuable way of opening up new learning directions, and will certainly increase the student's stock of knowledge. However, this alone will not usually suffice to provide a resolution to the problem, which is after all what faculty and fellow students (and the mythical board of directors in the company described in the case) are waiting anxiously to hear.

Finally, there is the *value-adding approach*, which seeks to go beyond a simple resolution of the problem and find ways and means of growing or advancing the company. An example might be recommending the adoption of a radically new market, product or strategy. The name means that the student is attempting not just to resolve the issue described but to use background information and his or her own analysis to come up with new ideas that will improve the company's situation still further.

This is the most difficult approach, and should probably not be attempted until one is familiar with the basics of the course in question. In other words, don't try to run before you can walk. But if you feel confident, by all means attempt this approach. Again, though, it is important not lose sight of the basic problems and issues of the case. It may do little good to recommend the introduction of a marvellous new product if the production system is incapable of making even the existing one.

In order to carry this approach off successfully, recommendations must *realistic* and *feasible*. Pie-in-the-sky approaches will win neither the plaudits of colleagues nor good marks from faculty.

Although there are three separate approaches, in practice the best idea may be to attempt a synthetic approach which combines features of all three. Clearly, as noted above, it is nearly always necessary to adopt a problem-solving approach in the first instance, to deal with the immediate issues confronting the company. But in terms of learning, the best value may be in going beyond the basic issues. Adopting a further learning approach can give opportunities for knowledge acquisition, while looking for ways to add value can be a useful exercise in knowledge use.

Case studies and benefit maximization

There is little further to be said on this subject, except to add that each case study ought to be exploited as far as possible for opportunities for learning, both from the information and ideas contained in the case and from any opportunities for further learning which may arise. Cases are ultimately learning tools, not puzzle-solving exercises.

Although they are to some extent didactic, business case studies are almost never black-white, right-wrong exercises. It is rare that there is only one potential resolution; there will always be different ways to approach the problem. Even if many of one's initial ideas turn out to be unworkable, this is not a problem; there is as much to be learned in the process of weeding out unfeasible ideas as there is in the generation of feasible ones.

Each case should do more than provide the knowledge of how to solve a particular problem or set of problems; it should also expand knowledge more generally, encourage creative thinking and broaden personal horizons. With these goals in mind, each case study resolved can become a contribution towards personal learning growth.

Case studies and knowledge management

One of the great assets of case studies is that they are in effect small, largely discrete exercises in knowledge management. The stages described above correspond to three stages of knowledge management. In the course of a case analysis, the student will go through this cycle of knowledge management several times.

The first two stages, the read-throughs or first and second viewings, are knowledge acquisition activities. The knowledge acquired thus is first organized and structured through the process of building up the picture of what the case presents, and is then put to use along with other, previously acquired knowledge in analysing the problem.

Then comes another round of knowledge acquisition and creation: when the available information is assessed any blanks are filled in through further research or assumptions. This knowledge is structured again, and is put to use a second time when first defining potential resolutions. Testing resolutions involves returning to one's stocks of knowledge again, and can even involve still further knowledge acquisition or creation. Finally, knowledge of the situation is used in arriving at a judgement as to which resolution is the best or most workable.

Case studies, then, are first and foremost mental exercises for the student. Although the most obvious aim, required by the situation, is to find a resolution to the problem posed by the case study, the real value comes through the exercise, through the acquisition, organization and use of knowledge. As preparation for real life analysis and decision making, they thus have great value.

Conclusions

This chapter has suggested methods for analysing a case, drawing out the relevant information and discarding the red herrings, getting to the heart of the problem and developing a solution. Its main suggestions are to look for multiple solutions or alternative scenarios – never assume there is just one right answer – and try to go beyond the bare facts of the case, by doing further research or even just using the imagination, to extend the possibilities as far as they will go.

Chapter 5

Working in teams
Creating value from synergy

Knowledge in itself is power.
Sir Francis Bacon

Team working was one of the business mantras of the 1990s. All sorts of new phrases were added to the management lexicon, like group working, team management and group decision making. Prompted by a somewhat overdue revelation that large modern businesses were becoming too complex for one person to control, theorists began working on how to manage the transition from an old-style autocratic form of organization to one where responsibility was devolved to more people.

In doing so, theorists were to some extent just catching up with reality. Businesses have always worked as teams to a considerable extent, with each member of the group depending on others to get their own job done. Plenty of comparisons can be drawn with other types of organization, such as sports teams, military units and symphony orchestras. In each of these cases, the individual members of the group have no chance to achieve their objective or aim, but they can do so when working together as a team, unit or orchestra. So it is with businesses.

That being said, team working is not as easy as it seems. Businesses are essentially groups of people, and people are individual and unique, each with their own foibles, quirks and idiosyncracies as well as talents, skills and competences. Some people naturally work well together, others have to make more of an effort. An understanding of the basics of group dynamics is probably the first essential when undertaking team work.

This chapter looks at some of these dynamics in the specific context of team work/study in the context of MBA programmes. Full-time students will nearly always be involved in one such group, and often in several for different courses or projects. Part-time/Executive MBA students will usually be involved in teams as well, though often of a slightly different nature; for example, their project work might involve putting together a team of colleagues from work. Distance learners may have less opportunity, but there may still be opportunities to put together ad hoc teams of fellow students, work colleagues and so on.

Many readers will already have had some experience of team working. This chapter may still be relevant however, as it suggests ways of managing teams on an equitable basis and of ensuring that teams reach their goals. Maximizing value comes through seeing those goals reached and ensuring that all members of the team benefit equally. Knowledge management skills are expanded and developed through a special subset of the discipline, *team knowledge management*.

Why do it?

Basically, there are three good reasons for undertaking MBA course work in teams, and it is for a combination of these reasons that most business schools are so keen on it:

- to achieve more inputs in terms of knowledge and ideas
- to achieve synergy through combining the talents of several people
- to replicate more accurately the real life management environment

The first point is often described as 'two heads are better than one'. If this is so, then three are usually better still, and so on. Actually, it is not quite as simple as that. Simply adding more people regardless of whether they are suited for the team in question does not necessarily add more value, and if too many people are involved the team is likely to sink under its own weight. Four to six people is the ideal size for a team (anything bigger is a committee). Ideally, too, everyone on the team should have something to contribute to it. In the environment of an MBA programme this is seldom a problem, as everyone is there for the same purpose.

The concept of team synergy is harder to explain, although the point made above, that only by combining their efforts can team members achieve their goals, is one aspect of the issue. But if the team is working efficiently – and this is a big *if* – the quality of decision making and implementation that comes out of it will be of signficantly better quality than the individual efforts of even its most talented members. The football team's star striker may be a player of great skill, but unless he has a similarly talented midfielder feeding him the ball, he will not realize his own potential. The conductor of the orchestra may be a leading expert on Beethoven, but without effective support from an excellent first violinist she will not be able to produce the best possible performance from the orchestra.

In effect, team working demonstrates that the whole is greater than the sum of its parts. Or at least, it has the potential to be.

Potential problems in team working

The discussion above refers to teams that work effectively. Very often, of course, they do not. Two of the most common problems are deadlock and groupthink.

Deadlock occurs when two or more members of the team take up apparently irreconcilable positions. When this happens, one of two things often occurs. The disagreement may persist until the team collapses with nothing being accomplished. More usually, to save face all around, a 'fudge' occurs, a compromise which both parties feel they can live with, but which satisfies neither and very often makes matters worse than they had been before.

Groupthink is a phenomenon whereby the members of a group, consciously or subconsciously, set out with the primary aim of finding a solution which meets the interests of all members, regardless of whether this is actually the best solution in the circumstances. Decisions made by groupthink are never better than second best (and are often rather worse). Groupthink makes everyone feel good, but it does not generate good ideas.

We deal with both these issues and how to resolve them when discussing group dynamics below.

The third point, that team working on the MBA is good preparation for later managerial work, is a valid one and worth bearing in mind. The simple position is that 'this is how managers work so we may as well start practising now'. But teams are also great generators of knowledge, as we shall discuss below, and developing team management skills more fully is a crucial part of the MBA experience.

Organizing teams

In some courses and programmes team members are assigned automatically, but in other cases students will be able to choose their own teams. Where the option exists, look where possible to include people from a number of different backgrounds into the team, to get a variety of perspectives on whatever problems and issues the team will be tackling. There will always be a temptation to pick team members on the basis of whether you get along with them personally. This is important – good personal relationships usually make for easy working relationships – but it should not be the only or even the primary factor.

Once the team members have been assigned or selected, it is recommended that they get to know one another before settling down to work. If time is short, just get together for a drink or a cup of coffee. Introduce yourselves, talk about your backgrounds and interests, learn what points you have in common. You do not need to become lifelong friends, but friendly personal relations will reduce some of the frictions that may result when the team begins to work in earnest.

Once the team is ready to begin working, the first step should always be to agree on a common purpose. Every member of the team needs to understand and buy into this goal. If you think some members are merely passively following the lead set by more dominant members, halt the process for a moment, go back and ensure the quieter members really are on side. They may just be reticent; or they may have real disagreements but be reluctant to mention them. If so, the latter need to be sorted out.

Next, it is recommended that any necessary tasks and roles be assigned. If the project is going to be a long or complex one, one member of the group should volunteer to act as a *rapporteur*.

He or she should take rough notes of the meeting, including any decisions made, action points set, tasks assigned and deadlines. These notes should be circulated as rough minutes after each meeting. This can be a very useful device for reminding team members of what has been agreed and where responsibilities lie.

You may feel more comfortable assigning the role of chairman to one member and asking him or her to convene and chair meetings, but in small work teams this should not be necessary. Discussions should be informal in nature, allowing for a free flow and interchange of ideas and comments. Anyone who even mentions *Roberts' Rules of Order* should be told off to buy the next round of drinks.

The functioning of the team

I will not give any rules, even general ones, for how teams should achieve their goals, because it is important that groups should be allowed to develop their own style and do things their own way. Achieving the goal is what is important; how you get there is of second-most importance, at best. As long as the team keeps focused on the goal and its members work efficiently together, then it should achieve its aims.

There are however two guiding principles which are important. The first is to make sure that every member of the team makes a contribution. If individual team members are allotted tasks, these should be spread as evenly as possible. In discussions of case studies, projects and so on, make sure everyone's voice is heard. In this way, you will get the best out of the team as a whole, and the individuals will be satisfied that they have made their contribution to the final result.

The second, related point is that everyone should have an equal chance for learning. When new concepts or ideas are introduced, make sure the whole team understands them and their implications. It may be necessary to carry some members along at first. Avoid the temptation to simply convince them of the rightness of your argument; rhetorical brilliance will do no one any favours at this point. If the ideas are good ones, they will do their work for you.

WHO MADE HIM TEAM LEADER...?

Ultimately, whether teams function successfully is down to (a) the personalities of the individuals in the team and (b) whether those personalities can work efficiently together. The next two sections of this chapter deal with these two points in turn.

The role of individual personality

One of the most common mistakes made by neoclassical economists (in my view, anyway) is to assume that all people are rational maximizers. That is, in any given situation, people will work to achieve the greatest possible good for themselves. This view ignores the fact that people are often irrational according to various motives. Altruism and generosity lead to apparent irrationality, as do errors resulting from faulty information, fatigue, compromises and 'fudging', or just plain stupidity. (There are books on this issue relating to management, but two eminently readable books on military psychology, Dixon's *The Psychology of Military Incompetence* (mentioned in Chapter 2) and Barbara Tuchman's *The March of Folly: From Troy to Vietnam*, illustrate beautifully how people make a mess of otherwise rational decisions.)

The problem is that in any given situation we tend to work not just to maximize utility but also to gratify our own egos, and sometimes the latter wins out over the former. This is particularly common in social situations, where ingrained patterns of behaviour can cause otherwise rational people to exhibit some quite ridiculous behaviours. Fatigue, too much caffeine and other background factors can further cloud judgement.

So it is in team working situations. Personality is always a factor in teams, and it is useless to pretend it is not. A better approach is to recognize the strengths and weaknesses of individual personalities. As there is not space here for a detailed technical discussion of this subject, let us illustrate the subject instead by describing a few archetypal teamworking personalities.

Teamworking personalities

People react to social pressures – such as those imposed by working in teams – in different ways, and their responses to these situations will differ. Although I have argued that getting to know team members before settling down to work is valuable, this is because better personal relations usually lead to easier working. Personalities and behaviours exhibited in social situations are not always the same as those exhibited in professional situations. People assume different things are being expected of them, and change their behaviours accordingly.

The ten archetypes which follow relate to team working personalities or workplace behaviours; they do not relate to overall personality. There is nothing terribly scientific about them; they are, frankly, a bit of fun. They illustrate the kinds of diverse personalities that one can find in a team. The chances are that when you sit down with your colleagues you will be able to identify some of these in the group.

Ten archetypes

Bull. Bulls are strong and impetuous, and tend to attack problems frontally. Their assets are great energy and a refusal to be daunted by the task that lies ahead. All problems have a solution, and usually all you have to do is throw enough time, energy, resources, etc. at the issue to see it through. They tend to lack finesse, and overlook some of the more subtle issues, which means they can be tripped up. Their energy and enthusiasm can be infectious, but equally can be annoying if unconstrained. In their headlong rush at the problem, they tend to pull weaker members of the team along with them.

> *Bulls are fond of saying:* 'No problem. We can sort this out. All we have to do is...'
> *Potential future career*: corporate raider

Mouse. Mice are industrious and hard workers, but in group situations they tend to sit quietly and say nothing. They are often exacting and professional in their approach to a task, and when set a task they deliver the appropriate results on time. In group discussions, however, they tend to sit back and let the conversation flow around them, not speaking even if they might have something valuable to contribute. Mice need to be brought out of themselves and into the discussion, and given time to organize their thoughts and speak; many do not handle pressure well. A great asset to a team, they need careful handling.

Mice are fond of saying: 'Oh, I'm sorry. Were you asking me?'
Potential future career: Internet millionaire

Rooster. The rooster likes to be visible and in a position of authority. They are usually good communicators and make excellent presenters; if you have a rooster in your team, consider using him or her to take the lead in classroom presentations. Roosters are also usually clever and have valuable opinions to contribute, particularly when it comes to how ideas will be received by their target audience. They can cause difficulties; some are genuine show-offs, which can irritate other members of the team, and they can be somewhat domineering. Properly managed, though, a rooster can be a valuable asset, especially when your team is competing with others.

Roosters are fond of saying: 'Let me do the talking.'
Potential future career: chairman of a multinational advertising firm

Tiger. Tigers are highly intelligent and good analysts. They tend to sit watchfully while others take their turn and present their ideas; then, when they see a mistake, they pounce suddenly, crushing their opposition (bulls and roosters are their favourite targets). Although this can be useful in that it can save the team from making its mistakes publicly, it can still be irritating. Nevertheless, tigers are great value. Their analytical abilities are important, and they tend to be good strategists. The real trick to managing them is to get them to say what *they* are thinking, not their views on other people's ideas.

Tigers are fond of saying: 'I think you'll find you've overlooked one small but important detail...'
Potential future career: management consultant

Monkey. Monkeys are clever and energetic and are often good intuitive thinkers, a trait which sometimes allows them to jump ahead of the rest of the team. They come up with a variety of original ideas (not all of which are always very practical, it must be said). They also tend to generate these ideas in a seemingly random order, which can be confusing for anyone trying to work through a project methodically. Monkeys can be a tremendous asset to a work team through the sheer volume and creativity of their thinking, but they need to work with the team, not outside it.

Monkeys are fond of saying: 'I've just come up with a better idea...'
Potential future career: director of research and development

Bee. Bees are diligent workers, industrious as one would expect, and are productive and good analysts. They tend to leave leadership to others, however, and are sometimes less than assertive in group discussions. Although capable of great focus and concentration, they can also lose focus and dissipate their efforts, and often rely on the support of a group to keep them going in the right direction. Bees are generally group-oriented and make excellent members of any team.

Bees are fond of saying: 'I've been working on this, and here are the notes I've made.'
Potential future career: senior analyst

Rabbit. Rabbits are very productive (no jokes, please) but tend to haste and disorganization. Once they focus on a subject, rabbits can do a lot of work quickly, and will come up with many good ideas and pieces of information. There is a tendency to do things at the last minute, and poor organizational skills mean many rabbits don't achieve as much as they might. Most are always trying to do better, however, and on the plus side they are enthusiastic and full of energy.

Rabbits are fond of saying: 'I'm late, I'm late, I'm very very late' [with apologies to Lewis Carroll]
Potential future career: director of human resource management

Squirrel. Squirrels are collectors and hoarders of information. They are the people who can seemingly produce any required piece of information at the drop of a hat, or at least know where to get it at short notice. Quick and industrious, squirrels can be an asset to any team. Their main drawback is their tendency to take on too much work; incapable of saying no when asked to do a job, they also volunteer for things which they probably won't be able to complete on time. In team situations, they need to be nudged into making sure they are working within their own limits.

> *Squirrels are fond of saying*: 'Yes, I'll do that.'
> *Potential future career*: fund manager

Sloth. Sloths are the opposite of rabbits; they are 'last-minuters', who never do anything until it is beyond urgent. Incapable of understanding the need for haste, they can be maddening to work with. This said, when they *do* get down to work, they usually produce what is required quickly and to a high quality standard; their lack of surface activity often conceals a very active brain. Other members of the team can try to convert sloths to a different way of thinking, or it might be best to let them work in their own way and make allowances in the team's schedule.

> *Sloths are fond of saying*: 'What's the rush? The deadline isn't until tomorrow.'
> *Potential future career*: director of strategic planning

Dodo. Dodos are, fortunately, very rare in most MBA programmes, as selection processes have become good at weeding them out, but a few still slip through. Dodos are not stupid, but like their namesake they are simply incapable of evolution (and probably in danger of extinction). Rigid thinkers, they find it difficult to accept new ideas, and they do so only slowly. Dodos can work hard and be industrious, but they need a lot of support and encouragement from the rest of the team.

> *Dodos are fond of saying*: 'That's impossible.'
> *Potential career*: politician

Functioning in groups

As the archetypes presented above show, any group is likely to have a mix of personalities and talents. Each member will have his or her individual strengths; nearly all will also have their individual weaknesses. At first sight, the members of the group may even appear incompatible.

In fact, getting a team to work well is a bit like doing a jigsaw puzzle, or perhaps better, like building a gearbox. Each piece has a place and will fit, but it can take a while to work out exactly where that place is. In most cases, though, with goodwill on all sides, it is possible to find a place for each and to make the whole work smoothly and without friction.

As I said above, I don't believe there are any hard and fast rules for making teams work *effectively*. The mesh of different personalities and abilities means that each team functions in a unique way. There are, however, some guidelines for making sure that teams work *efficiently*. The three most important of these are as follows.

1   Stay focused on the goal. It is very easy for group discussions to wander off topic. If the group is headed in that direction, someone needs to gently nudge them back on course. Sometimes a little leeway can be given; if someone feels strongly about something and wants to get it off his or her chest, let him or her have his or her way for a bit. But remember that the group's energies and resources are finite, and the goal is what matters. Concentrate, and don't lose track of the objective.

2   Communicate clearly. In group discussions, say what you mean concisely and without rhetorical flourishes. Ensure that your colleagues understand you and follow your ideas. If one or more members of the team speak English as a second language, stick to plain English; avoid elaborate metaphors or local slang which can confuse. In written communications (see also Chapter 6), be concise and stick to the point. At all costs, be sure that everyone in the group is working from the same information. If one member learns something that is useful to the group's objective, he or she should let the others know. Again, it is recommended that

notes be kept of group discussions and circulated as aides-memoire to all members.

3   Show respect for all members of the group at all times. Be careful about matters such as timekeeping; do not be late for meetings and do not waste your colleagues' time. Do not talk down to people just because they may seem slow in following your ideas (they may not be able to follow because you may in fact be wrong). Be inclusive, and bring people into the discussion if they appear to be getting lost. Let everyone have his or her say, taking it in turns if necessary. Above all, never lose your temper (unless this is a calculated move when negotiating some point, and even then this is something of a Doomsday weapon).

Showing respect for other members of the group may just seem like good manners, but in fact, self-interest is also involved. Mutual respect between members of the group serves to oil the wheels of its internal machinery; the group will work more smoothly and be more productive. Better results will be achieved, and more learning and greater benefits will accrue to all parties.

Failure to agree

Most groups that fail to achieve their objective (in which category I include unsuitable compromises and 'fudges') do so because members are unable to agree on some key issue. Deadlock is quite likely to occur at some point in any group's activities, and it is well to be prepared for this beforehand.

When deadlock does occur, the first rule is to keep calm. It is at this point that, depending on the nature of the people involved, tempers may flare. Keep them in check; be prepared to act as peacemaker if necessary. Make sure everyone is calm and ready to discuss the matter before proceeding.

Get both sides to explain their thinking clearly. Ensure that they can support their own position as well as critique the opposition. One useful tactic is to get each side to critique their own position; look at the ideas they are defending and describe what may be wrong with them. Under this kind of self-examination, apparently inflexible positions tend to crumble. But if people are changing their views, they must do so because they genuinely believe change is possible; compromise, as discussed below, is usually the wrong move.

If deadlock persists, review the options. Most deadlocks occur in what look like black and white situations; one side has taken one view, the other side has taken the opposing view, and neither will shift. Now is the time to review other positions and look for a third option.

It is always tempting in such situations to compromise, to look for a 'grey' position between the two and find something that both parties can live with. Think hard before doing this. Compromises are often unsatisfactory in terms of results; they tend to be inefficient and weak solutions, largely because they are cobbled together out of parts of two apparently conflicting ideas. Compromise is often worse than no decision at all, and it is amazing how many bad business decisions have been made down the years (centuries?) by people looking for compromise solutions. Also, compromises also often result in one side, or both, giving up some deeply held principle, and this can cause bad feeling, now or later.

A better way is to *innovate an entirely new solution*. That is, when faced with a deadlock, find a third option which is better than the two currently on the table. (If deadlock has ensued, it is entirely likely that neither proposed solution is a good one; otherwise, why would the other party be so opposed?) This is, of course, easier said than done. On the other hand, the prospect of deadlock and failure should prove a spur to more creative thinking. Look for a breakthrough. Turn around, examine the problem again, and come at it from a different angle. If that fails, keep trying.

Last of all, if other measures have failed, consider allowing the dissenters to write or present their own ideas as a minority view (the dissenters will, obviously, be in a minority; otherwise they would not be dissenters). If this is necessary, do it with dignity and respect for both parties. If the team is presenting in class, make it clear that there is no bad feeling between the parties (lie if you have to). There are few things worse than seeing a team presenting a report when clearly some members disagree with the results and are angry and upset about it. This is embarrassing and distracting for everyone.

Some dos and don'ts for working in teams

do:

- get to know your colleagues personally and develop good relationships with them
- ensure that all members of the team contribute equally
- keep records of discussions, even just in point form
- stay focused on the team's goals
- show respect for your colleagues
- communicate your views and ideas clearly and directly

don't:

- hold back information if it will be useful to the group
- talk down to others if they appear not to be following you
- be late for meetings or miss meetings without giving notice
- lose your temper, especially not in front of people from outside the group

Benefit maximization

This chapter has gone on quite long enough, and I just want to add a few comments on how getting a team to work well can maximize the benefits accruing from an MBA programme.

First, the experience of working in teams is excellent preparation for future careers in management. Anybody can be a member of a team. Getting that team to function as efficiently and effectively as possible is another matter. Use the experience of team working on the MBA not only to produce the required results, but to study group dynamics in action and work on ways of improving your own team management skills. Don't take teams for granted; study them as they work, and think of ways in which they could improve their working methods.

Second, and related to the above, the experience of working in teams will strengthen your communications skills. The need to express yourself clearly and concisely to a varied audience is one aspect of this; so too is the need to listen, absorb and respond to the views of others. Doing all this with respect, allowing others to have their say and creating a climate of fairness is important. So is creating a climate in which everyone feels comfortable about expressing their views. There is much more to communication than just speaking or writing.

Third, working with fellow students in teams should begin to show how teams function in terms of generating knowledge and creating synergy. A good team is much greater than just the sum of its parts; it can achieve things that no individual could dream of (or at least, do much more than dream of). Understanding a little of how this process works is a major benefit to be derived from the MBA experience.

Knowledge management

Teams are essentially tools for generating and using knowledge. Like networked computers, or like a sort of collective 'super-brain', they take in knowledge inputs from all members of the team, analyse them, and make the results available to all members to use, individually or collectively.

Team members acquire knowledge and feed it into the team, but through mutual discussion and analysis, teams also create knowledge; indeed, this is one of their greatest strengths. Teams do not have collective memories as such, only the memories of their individual members, and this is a potential weakness. However, this weakness can be overcome if the team members store knowledge they have acquired and generated in notes and databases (it is for this reason that I reiterate the need for teams to keep records). Finally, when using knowledge, teams working together have a longer reach and greater capability than any individual member, provided always that the team is working smoothly and harmoniously. To go back to the head of the chapter, a football team, an infantry platoon and a symphony orchestra all function because they are combining the knowledge and use outputs of all members of the team.

Conclusions

Teams are an essential part of modern management. A complex but very readable and interesting account of team working and knowledge management can be found in Ikujiro Nonaka and Hirotaka Takeuchi's *The Knowledge-Creating Company* (Oxford: Oxford University Press, 1995), and this is strongly recommended. In terms of MBA programmes, the experience of team working is one of the most important and valuable benefits the programme provides. Students can maximize this by studying and analysing how teams work and looking for ways to make them work better. Possession of good team working skills is an asset that is likely to always have currency.

Chapter 6

Written communication
Who writes, wins

Writers, like teeth, are divided into incisors and grinders.
Walter Bagehot

An odd thing happened in the 1990s: writing came back into fashion. The agent responsible for this trend was e-mail, which suddenly exploded onto the scene as a complement to, and increasingly a substitute for, the telephone. Requests for face-to-face meetings or telephone conversations to explain an idea to a superior increasingly draw the answer: 'Send me an e-mail.'

MBA programmes often don't stress the importance of written communication as much as they might. Some faculty are prepared to accept written reports and case study write-ups no matter how many grammatical and spelling errors they may contain. Fair enough, you may say; if the professor will accept it as it is, why should you waste your time doing more?

The answer is simple but important: writing is a form of inter-personal communication, and learning to write effectively is an important part of the whole package of communications skills. Just because faculty at your business school are prepared to accept written work of a quality that would probably make your high school English teacher feel faint is no reason to sell yourself short in this department.

The good, the bad and the ugly

Consider the following three e-mails, drawn from a real-life example, received by one manager from three of his colleagues. Which makes most sense to you? To which would you respond most favourably?

dear jim
just heard the latest qtrly reports are about out, suggest we might have a few problems. could I talk to you soonest about my depts requirments ,let me kkno when we can meet up
mike

Dear Jim
I understand the quarterly budget report is to be circulated on Friday. I have been going over my department's books, and I think I can make a case for some more money to be invested in our area. I'd like to meet and discuss my plans in more detail. When would be convenient?
Yours,
Andrew Robinson

Dear Jim
I have just found out that our business unit's quarterly budget report is about to be circulated to all departments, I think on Friday but I cannot be sure. If you have any further details on this, perhaps you could let me know. Anyway, my reason for writing is that we have been doing a considerable amount of research in my department for several months now, and we feel that if we are going to move further towards our target goals, then we will need to ask for some further capital expenditure. Is there anyway we could discuss this situation in more detail and present our views to you? If possible, a meeting might be arranged so that you and I could talk this through in more detail. Do please let me know when you might be available to attend such a meeting.
Yours
Anne Cartwright

Discussing these, the manager who received them told me, 'I instinctively responded to Andrew first, I don't know why. Anne and Mike are perfectly competent managers, but I felt I didn't have time to decode Anne's e-mail or decipher Mike's. So I'm seeing Andrew first.'

Good writing is important for its discipline, and sloppy writing is sometimes a sign of sloppy thinking. But much more important is the impact that good writing can have on an audience. 'Selling' your ideas to colleagues and senior managers, or to customers, is critical to career success, and often that selling has to be done in writing. To repeat, writing is one form of interpersonal communication. And in an economy that is increasingly becoming dominated by knowledge, the ability to communicate knowledge is only barely of secondary importance to knowledge itself. In the twenty-first century, victory goes to the communicators.

One way and another, MBA students have to do quite a lot of writing. There are case write-ups and reports, project reports and other assigned work. There is e-mail contact with fellow students and faculty. There are notes taken in class and while doing desk or field research that have to be structured and ordered, and there are notes from meetings referred to in the previous chapter. There are written outlines for oral presentations.

De-mystifying writing

Many people find writing difficult, and many otherwise confident men and women are uneasy about their perceived inability to write well. In part, they are daunted by writing's supposed mystique. Writing is perceived as an 'art'; when we think of writing we think of Shakespeare, Molière, Tolstoy, Basho, Cao Xuequin, the great canonical writers of ages past.

But most writing is not like that, any more than most personal verbal communication is like the work of Demosthenes or Winston Churchill. Most of the time, we are simply trying to get a message across at a fairly ordinary level.

Writing itself is a skill. The best way to develop it is to practise it; given time, anyone can become a competent writer. Above all, don't get bound up in the 'creative' aspect of writing. There is creativity involved, but it happens in the mind, in the creation, structuring and ordering of ideas. Writing is a mechanical process by which those ideas are recorded and disseminated – nothing more.

All writing seems burdensome at the time one is doing it, but it can also be an opportunity to develop and refine written communication skills. This chapter explains some of the basic principles of professional writing, in particular the application of the principle of fitness for purpose. It looks at the three primary elements of writing – structure, style and content – in general terms, and then discusses the application of these elements to forms of writing most commonly required of MBA students. The principal argument is that by becoming more effective writers, students will become more effective communicators generally. Writing is an important tool in knowledge management, and developing writing skills effectively increases managerial potential.

Fitness for purpose

There are very few hard and fast rules in writing. One of the most important of those few, however, is that all writing should be *fit for its purpose*. That is, it should be capable of communicating the intended message to the intended audience, and all its elements – structure, style and content – should be geared to that end. When a piece of writing is finished, subsequent reading and editing should aim to eliminate anything that is not relevant to the document's purpose.

The simplest way of assessing fitness for purpose is to test any writing against the following:

- does the work clearly and completely express the writer's own *aims*?
- will it be intelligible to and acceptable to its intended *audience*?
- does it communicate fully and completely the intended *message* to that audience?
- will it stimulate the desired *response* from that audience?

The acronym AAMR (aims, audience, message, response) can serve as a reminder of these points.

Aims

The first step, even before switching on the computer, is to be clear about one's own aims. What is the purpose of the communication? What is the author intending to say, and for what purpose? This sounds like simple common sense, but a surprising number of people begin writing *without* any such clear idea. The result can be confusing to read, especially when they apparently change their minds partway through the text.

Audience

Next, determine who the communication is addressed to. Try to picture them in your mind's eye. Do you know them personally, or are they strangers? Will only a few people read the communication, or is it for general distribution? How familiar will the audience be with the subject you intend to discuss? How and when are they likely to read the communication? Are they likely to be sympathetic to your aims, or will you need to convince them?

This again sounds like common sense, but getting the audience wrong is a major mistake made by many writers, even seasoned professionals. The key point to remember is to write *to the audience*. Writing is communication; and all communication requires two parties, a sender and a receiver. A written communication which the audience cannot understand is like a radio message sent out on the wrong frequency. Make sure you are connecting with the audience when writing.

Message

Message refers to the actual text and illustrations used. Decide what to say and to whom to say it; then decide *how* to say it. Use your knowledge of the audience to determine this; set your style, structure and content (see below) according to their needs. Remember that the audience has to read what you have written. Each sentence or illustration needs to convey a message to that audience. If when reading over the text again you cannot tell what the message is, cut the passage in question; if you don't know, your audience certainly won't.

Response

Finally, consider how you want your audience to respond. If the communication is for their information only, you will still want to make sure that they read, digest and store the information, so present the information in a way which makes this easy for them. If you want responses, such as comments or criticisms, or actions, from the audience, structure the work accordingly. For example, if you are writing a bid for funding and intend that your audience should react favourably (i.e. give you money), make sure the actual pitch is clearly put and in a prominent place in the document; this should be the central point of the document, and anything else included should merely be supporting or verifying information.

The AAMR model is a good way of keeping written communication focused. All written communications must pay attention to these four points. Missing one or getting one wrong means the communication could be misdirected: it could reach the wrong audience, or more commonly, reach the right audience but fail to be understood or to provoke the desired response.

A picture is worth a thousand words, but only if you can tell what the picture is

The AAMR model applies to visual as well as text presentations (a point which seems lost on the designers of most websites). Whether one is working with text or images, one is still trying to communicate a message to an audience, to get one's own aims across and provoke a response. Just as words, phrases and sentences need to be chosen with this idea in mind, so do visuals such as slides, photos and so on.

There is an additional difficulty in working with illustrative material, and this is the need to make sure the audience can interpret what they see. Illustrations are usually intended to simplify or illuminate, but often they end up being baffling and confusing. We all recognize words when they are put in front of us, and can read the literal meaning of a sentence even if we are not always sure what the author's intent may be. But illustrations often need interpretation. When using visual material, always pick simple, literal illustrations that show exactly what is intended (and preferably, nothing more).

Structure

How to structure a written communication is every bit as important as the style and content, and some structure decisions need to be made even before the latter are finally settled. Again, the structure of a message has to be fit for its purpose. There are obvious differences between a project report and an e-mail, but there are many more subtle gradations in between.

One of the time-honoured methods of structuring written communication, probably already familiar to most people, is 'Say what you are going to say, say it, then say what you have said.' In other words, introduce the topic concisely so that people have an idea of what they will be reading, then include the body of information on the topic, and then conclude by summarizing what the document has said. This may at first look repetitious, but the introduction and conclusion serve valuable purposes, not only in tying up the document when it is first read but as aides-memoire for later reference.

Introductions and conclusions should be brief. Introductions should summarize the content of the document, and any important sub-headings (see below) should be mentioned. The introduction should also summarize the theme of the document (that is, the author's aim in writing it). Conclusions should also be brief, and should bring out the main points that the author wishes the audience to take away with them. For most professional writing, it is quite acceptable and often helpful to use bullet points or lists when summarizing in this way, but don't feel bound by this. Finally, never put any piece of information in either introduction or conclusion which does not appear prominently in the body of the document.

The central portion of the document is of course the main content or 'meat' (see section on content, below). This is of course the most complex part of the document, where the information to be conveyed to the audience is located. There is a variety of devices in addition to plain text that can be used, including:

- sub-headings. These are terrific for breaking up the flow of text and introducing an obvious and visible structure, and good headings allow the reader to navigate easily around the text. But don't overuse them; don't put in a heading before each paragraph for example. Each heading ought to introduce one main sub-theme or group of ideas. Only in very long documents should you ever go below two levels of sub-heading (i.e. sub-headings and sub-sub-headings).

- tables. Much data, particularly numerical data, can be usefully summarized in tables positioned in the text. Be certain that tables are fully explained in the accompanying text, however, and alway check the numbers; for example, double-check that a column of percentages actually does add up to 100.
- illustrations. As with tables, they can be valuable explanatory tools, but be certain that they are clear and fully explained in the text.
- lists. Lists should be used fairly sparingly; if used less frequently, they will be all the more emphatic when they do appear. Use lists for action points and other strings of concepts which need to stand out from the text and be taken away by the reader.
- bullet points (like these). Less formal than lists, bullet points are a cheap and cheerful way of conveying information in bite-sized chunks. Use them for emphasis, and don't overdo it; reading an entire case write-up composed of strings of bullet points is less than fun for the reader.

Structuring communications for MBAs

Although as stated at the outset of the chapter, MBAs will probably be involved in writing a wide variety of communications; for reasons of space I will concentrate here on five of the most common:

E-mail messages: Although we now depend it on like we depend on oxygen, e-mail has to be one of the ugliest forms of communication known to humanity. No one enjoys reading e-mail (well, all right, but if you do, keep it quiet). E-mail messages need to be as brief as possible, with no wasted words or space. Introduction and conclusion are important for longer mails, but should probably be a single sentence at most. Attach graphics or longer attachments if you must, but clearly state what is attached and what the reader is supposed to do with it. Remember, your e-mail is one in what may be a queue of fifty or a hundred which has built up since the reader last logged on; short, simple e-mails which are easy to understand and respond to will create more of an effect.

Case writeups: As mentioned in Chapter 4, case write-ups should normally be 2-3 pages, although some faculty will have other preferences; always find out before beginning your first write-up. If the specified preference is 2-3 pages, stick to those parameters; write-ups of two paragraphs or twenty pages will be equally unwelcome. Don't use illustrative material unless you absolutely must or the case instructions call for it, though tables with figures are acceptable (especially, obviously, in finance or accounting cases). Use short paragraphs with simple sentences. Bullet points and lists are good ways of summarizing key issues quickly, but don't overdo it.

Project reports: These of course are much longer, and are probably the most complex form or writing most MBAs will undertake, whether referring to in-class projects or real projects with companies (see Chapter 9). Think carefully about the structure of these before beginning. Arrange your information and notes beforehand, and making a detailed outline is recommended. For each point in the outline, consider whether illustrative material or tables could be used and where. Make sure the introduction and conclusion follow the guidelines given above; consider the option of writing both these last, once the body of the report is finished. Remember that much of your audience is likely to be less familiar with the subject matter of your report, and structure it so the material is easy to follow.

Minutes and notes: These should be as short as possible, conveying the maximum infomation in the minimum number of words. Use some sort of list structure, such as legal format for longer documents, or lists or even bullet points for shorter ones. The reader will want to be able to read these in a very few minutes, and brevity is the most important structural feature. Introduction and conclusion are useful as statements of purpose, but should rarely be longer than a sentence.

Personal research notes: As you are the audience as well as the communicator for these, it is important to write/compile them in a way which you will find easy to read and digest later. These are contributions to your own personal stock of knowledge;

organize the knowledge thus acquired in a way which will make it easy to use later.

Style

A lot of people talk a lot about style for written communication in management, and most of it is not very helpful. In fact, the rules for style are exactly the same as for structure: fitness for purpose. First, write in a style with which you are comfortable and in which you are capable; don't reach for rhetorical flourishes which are beyond your ability, but don't dumb down your text either. Second, as the examples below will show, the style may need to vary depending on the type of communication and the intended audience. Write to your audience; write in such a way so that they will understand and respond.

Many people may attempt to give you advice about what style to adopt, and most of them should be ignored. Particularly, ignore the language fascists, who tell you not to split infinitives or end sentences with prepositions. Violating both these rules is perfectly possible and in some cases may be desirable, so long as this is the best possible way to convey meaning and message. Second, ignore the current trend, which is for short sentences. 'Sentences should be as short as possible', one authority on this subject has declared. If this were so, most management documents and reports would read like Dr Seuss. Above all, I recommend you do *not* rely on the grammar checkers which many word-processing software packages now feature. Apart from the fact that many of these are full of errors themselves, using them religiously produces writing of a singular monotony, full of sentences of uniform length and word count, making documents as whole dull and difficult to read.

As noted above, find a style with which you are comfortable and which you like writing. Stay focused on the needs of the audience; do the words which you have used adequately convey your meaning? Pretend you are a complete stranger, entirely ignorant of the subject under discussion; would you be able to understand what is being written? If not, perhaps it is time to consider some revision.

Long sentences and words *in general* are not a good idea, because usually there is a shorter and clearer way of expressing the same idea. William Faulkner was famous for writing sentences that would go on for a page or more, but most of us are not Faulkner; usually, we can say what we mean rather more concisely. But if the idea is a complex one, it may need a longer sentence.

Many people are afraid of writing because they believe they are writing in the 'wrong' way, and silly rules about style only complicate the matter. When engaging in written communication, you should be free to adopt whatever devices you know and can use, *provided* they achieve the ultimate aim of effective communication with the reader. Writing is one of the few places where you can actually be yourself. Develop your own effective style, and enjoy using it. By expressing yourself *as yourself*, you will probably make more of an impact.

Sentences and paragraphs

Most people actually write quite good sentences, as long as they remember to include things like verbs and nouns, and above all, punctuation (remember the famous case of 'King Charles the First walked and talked half an hour after his head was cut off'; insert a full stop at some point in this sentence, and you get a rather different meaning). Paragraphs are another matter.

Paragraphs are effectively a form of structure. Each paragraph include a group of related sentences, all of which focus on one particular subject (people say you should not have paragraphs of only one sentence, but that can be ignored as well). Paragraphs should not usually have more than one subject, and complex subjects may need two paragraphs. Use them to separate ideas from one another, and also for emphasis; don't insert a hard return just because it seems like it has been a while since the last one.

Style for MBAs

E-mail messages: style may not seem important here, but as the example given early in the chapter shows, style can play a role in getting a response to your e-mail. The best option is terse, to the point, with no wasted words or excess verbiage. I am talking here about e-mails sent on a professional basis; I exclude e-mails to friends and family, where you can of course waste as much of their time as you wish.

Case write-ups: because they are short and there is usually a lot of information to get through, case studies again need a fairly terse style. Concentrate on the message; the audience is likely to be limited to a few faculty and colleagues, and you will usually have a good idea of their requirements. The focus here should be on getting the message across clearly.

Project reports: longer and more complex, project reports allow more freedom to develop style; but again, remember to concentrate on the audience and the message. As we noted above, the style usually has to be sufficiently clear to explain complicated concepts to an audience that may be less familiar with them than you are yourself. Don't talk down to your audience, but beware of being too technical as well. Define and explain technical terms and be sure any tables or illustrative material are clearly explained as well.

Minutes and notes: style here should be as concise as possible. For informal notes, full sentences may not even be necessary; make your points one by one without flourish.

Personal notes: up to the individual, but in the interests of saving time, these should again be brief. They do have to be clear, though; remember, you will have to read them yourself later and be able to understand what they mean.

Content

It is impossible to generalize about content even to the extent we have about structure and style, as content must obviously be specific to the aim, audience, message and response desired. The following, though, can be used as general guidelines, especially for longer documents like case write-ups and reports.

1   Pay attention to the level of background material you include. 'Enough to be clear to the reader, but not so much as to bore them' is the best rule of thumb. Once you have written out the background section, read it through again. Does every detail you have included actually matter to the issue at hand? Does the fact that the marketing director is 54

years old have any relevance to the firm's present marketing problems? If you feel it does, keep it in; if it does not, delete the passage in question. Use background sections to build up a clear picture for the reader, who you must always assume knows less than you do (or at the very least, needs reminding).

2   Always back up your ideas with evidence, reference, facts. If the evidence seems doubtful in any way, say so plainly and indicate why you have chosen to use it. If you must speculate, indicate clearly where you are doing so, and why.

3   If you need to make assumptions due to missing information, do so clearly and at the outset.

4   If you have done a lot of research, resist the temptation to show off. Illuminate your writing with such results of the research as are relevant, and do not take the reader on a Cook's tour of your research programme. (Some academic journals could profit by this policy as well.)

5   Always check facts and names. If references are required, give them in full and be sure they are accurate.

6   Always assume that your report or work may be challenged by the reader, who will want to know why you have (or have not) included certain ideas or reached certain conclusions. *Be prepared to defend and discuss every word you have written.*

Knowledge management and written communication

If the arguments at the opening of this chapter concerning the importance of written communication were not convincing, here is another: writing is an important part of knowledge management. This is true whether the document being written is intended to record and store information (knowledge organization) or to communicate with others (knowledge use). Writing is in effect a channel (verbal communication being another), through which knowledge is managed. For these purposes, it does not really matter if that writing is on paper, on a computer, sent by e-mail or by post, or even scratched on a piece of birchbark with a sharp stick; it is still communication, and it still matters.

Too much information

Most people when sitting down to write for the first time worry about being able to fill a page. In fact, overwriting is the most common curse of professional writing. Most of the documents I see could be comfortably cut by one-half or more, with no loss of value to the reader. The most common problems are excess verbiage (sometimes sentences are too long, most often there are too many sentences), repetition (used sparingly, it can be a valuable tool for emphasis, but in much professional writing there is '*déja vu* all over again') and muddy or confused style which means that not only is the reader never entirely clear what is going on, but one suspects that the writer isn't either. Obfuscation takes up a lot of space; just listen to the long and complex sentences used by American presidential candidates in their speeches as an example. Clarity and brevity often go hand in hand.

There is another problem, of course, and that is the culture which has grown up in some quarters of management which actually values weighty documents over slimmer ones: a clear case of 'never mind the product, just feel the weight of our procedures manual'. A colleague of an analyst acquaintance decided to test the validity of this culture. Finishing off an immense report on the transport sector, he included a footnote at the bottom of about page 170: 'If you have read this far, call me [phone number included] for a free bottle of champagne.'

Needless to say he did not get a single call. Readers are left to draw their own conclusions about the effectiveness of this kind of written communication.

Those who cannot write so as to make themselves understood clearly are partially mute. They can acquire knowledge, but their ability to structure and use it will be severely impaired.

Some further tips

If writing comes only with difficulty, consider a few of the following devices which may help:

- When preparing to write, if possible, make sure you are physically comfortable and can work without interruption. Broken concentration is never good for writing.
- For any document of more than a few paragraphs, consider drafting an outline first to help get your thoughts in order. For longer reports, the outline can often serve as the basis of a contents list and/or executive summary, so this is not wasted effort.
- Consider writing the introduction and the conclusion last, once the body of the report is finished. That way all the ideas are down on paper, and it is often easier to introduce and summarize them.
- Very few people can produce perfect first drafts. Always read over what you have written and make amendments. For longer documents, allow a day or even more to consider what you have written and approach it again.
- Good writing usually sounds good. Read your drafts out loud, or to yourself; if something sounds wrong, you may need to do some revising.
- Especially for longer documents and formal reports and presentations, proofread your work carefully, looking for errors. It is advisable to do this on a printed copy; things do look different on paper from on screen.
- Don't rely on spellcheckers and other aids attached to word processing packages. Contrary to popular opinion, these are *not* infallible.

Maximizing benefits

Again, the point has been made so often in this chapter that there is no need for much further repetition. Having ideas is one thing; communicating them is another. Writing is one of the most important channels of communication. It follows that being able to write effectively is an important communications skill. Good writers are not necessarily good managers; but good managers are nearly always able to write to an acceptable standard.

The MBA programme requires a great deal of writing. Rather than seeing this as a chore to be got over, consider seeing it as valuable practice and an opportunity to develop writing skills. In professional terms, these may come into use even before the programme is over, when students begin marketing themselves to recruiters (see Chapter 12).

One of the core aims of most MBA programmes is to produce graduates who are able to communicate effectively. It follows that honing your writing skills is a key part of this. Use the MBA experience to learn how to make your writing work for you.

Conclusions

Written communication is only one aspect of communication, and the next chapter looks in more detail at the equally valuable skills connected with oral communication. But there is no doubt that writing is important for a manager, and is probably going to become even more important in the future. Good writing makes a favourable impression, and it can be critical in helping to sell ideas in competitive situations. The MBA programme should be used as an opportunity to hone and practise writing skills.

Two important points need to be reiterated about writing. First, be natural, following your own instincts about style and so on, but always keep the reader in mind. If the reader cannot follow or does not understand, your writing has been wasted. Second, don't treat writing as a mystical creative experience. The creative aspect of writing goes on in the mind, when ideas are being created and organized; the rest of it is a skill like any other.

Chapter 7

Working in the classroom
Managing presentations and discussions

I do not greatly care whether I have been right or wrong on any point, but I care a great deal about knowing which of the two I have been.
Samuel Butler

In most MBA programmes (apart, obviously, from distance learning programmes) the classroom is the crucible. Information is exchanged, analysed, synthesized and discussed. Questions are asked and opinions are challenged. A classroom which does all these things is one which is well managed by the teaching faculty, but it is also one where every student plays his or her part in the information exchange process. When this happens, when twenty or thirty people concentrate, focus, bend their knowledge and mental energies towards a problem, discuss it, argue over it, and finally develop an answer, the atmosphere can be stimulating and electrifying.

Oddly, though, the concept of the classroom as a focal point of learning has often been criticized. It is seen as being 'not practice-oriented', too remote from the 'real' world of business. Critics who voice these opinions are missing the point. It is the very separateness of the classroom which makes it so important. Away from the concerns and inhibitions of the workplace, students can be free to innovate and create, to work out solutions, to come up with new concepts; and yes, to fail from time to time. Getting it wrong in the classroom hurts no one and costs no one money, and it is all part of the learning process.

All three levels of knowledge management are present in such a classroom, and we will come back to this later. For the moment, the most important point to be stressed is *active learning*; that is, students proactively acquiring knowledge, not just waiting passively for it to be delivered to their desks. The interchange between students, and particularly between students and faculty, is the central channel through which learning takes place. Nearly all faculty (if I may say so, all the good ones) prefer it this way. There is nothing more dispiriting than trying to teach twenty or thirty people who simply sit and look silently back with blank faces, apparently unable to respond to what one is saying.

Distance learning: managing the virtual classroom

Students on distance learning MBAs, of course, have no physical classroom and therefore miss out on this particular channel of learning. Fortunately, e-mail has gone some way to compensating for this, and discussion groups and so on can be used to create a sort of 'virtual classroom' in which all the participants are in contact remotely.

This kind of communication takes more effort, because most of us find it hard to be as direct to people we cannot see and do not know personally. Then too, unlike the 'real' classroom where 99 per cent of all communication is oral, the 'virtual' classroom usually requires written communication (unless the programme uses some form of videoconferencing; not many do). On the other hand, the participants often have more time to think and frame their views; the instant response often required in a classroom discussion is missing.

This sort of device is still in its infancy, and every distance learning MBA I have seen still has kinks to be worked out in this respect. But the groundwork is there. It is harder working in a virtual classroom, but the benefits can still be reached.

I do not mean to make distance learning MBA students sound like second-class citizens; I have a lot of time for distance learning programmes and many of them are excellent in many ways. But it is important to be aware of the differences between these and classroom-based MBAs, and to compensate as far as possible for the loss of learning opportunities caused by the restrictions on human contact.

The stage and the players

The classroom *is* an artificial environment, and we can say that without any apology. To understand its dynamics, consider another artificial environment, the theatre. In effect, the classroom is a stage; the desks, lecterns, blackboards/whiteboards and computers and monitors are the props. The faculty and students are the players, improvising their own production as they go through each session. Teaching faculty additionally serve as directors, prompting when the production starts to slow down, providing the framework and the theme to which everyone works.

The role of faculty (reprised)

In Chapter 3, when discussing courses generally, we discussed how faculty design courses which are usually built around or derived from their own interests and research priorities. These courses are never complete pictures, but are rather the product of the faculty member's own views and ideas. Ideally, they are a framework on which students can hang further knowledge as and when they acquire it.

In Chapter 1, when introducing the idea of a resource-based MBA, we discussed faculty as having four important roles in terms of their relationships with students:

- intelligent agents, experts in the processing and use of knowledge;
- guides, whose function is to help students learn;
- possessors of specialist expertise and knowledge, the product of their own research and interests;
- independent minds, unbiased and judging what they see and hear impartially.

On the classroom 'stage', faculty will be exercising all four of these roles, usually simultaneously. Their job is not so much to teach as to *facilitate learning*. They do this by structuring and guiding classroom sessions, drawing on their own resources as intelligent agents and from their specialist expertise. When they ask questions or give opinions, it is with the goal of encouraging learning.

The standard tool whereby faculty communicated with students was formerly the lecture, supplemented by the case study. Lectures will be familiar to nearly all readers from their undergraduate days, and I can think of nothing new that needs to be added on this subject. Case studies were dealt with in detail in Chapter 4. Most faculty, however, now rely on group discussions and other forms of interaction which allow students to learn dynamically, and to learn from colleagues as well as from the teaching faculty. It is on this aspect of the classroom 'stage' that this chapter concentrates.

The students

Important to the concept of active learning in the classroom is the realization that there is not just one intelligent agent in the room, but twenty or thirty. Students will also have some specialist knowledge or experience, even if in some cases this is limited in scope. They thus possess two of the four qualities we ascribed to faculty.

Of the other two, independence of mind is something that can and should be cultivated. It is directly related to the opening up and broadening of personal horizons referred to in Chapter 2. By being receptive to new ideas, you are at the same time acquiring an independence of mind, as you are no longer relying on your preconceptions. In the classroom, independence of mind is vital because it will lead you to analyse, question and challenge, not just passively accept. And later in the business world, this same trait will be invaluable in analysing situations and making decisions.

The role of guide is primarily the province of teaching faculty; primarily, but not entirely. Faculty devise the course and set the framework for learning, but within that framework each student will have plenty of room for personal learning. Most obviously, students can take away what they hear and learn and explore further through independent research. But in the classroom, by analysing what is being said (or shown on screen), taking views, making points in discussion and asking questions, students are also guiding their own learning. (Some of the best classroom discussions I have ever witnessed were largely outside my control; I and my teaching colleagues simply stood on the sidelines, played referee if things got overheated, and (regretfully) drew it all to a close when it looked like we were running out of time. I enjoyed these occasions and learned from them, as did the students.)

Why should we have to do all the work?

Why should students have to be so proactive? After all, they are paying for the experience, and it is their fees that provide (part of) faculty salaries. Haven't they a right to expect value for money?

Of course they do, and a bad course – that is, one where little or no learning results – is not providing that value. But the experience of almost everyone who has gone through the MBA experience is that the 'bad' courses are the ones where there is little or no classroom interaction and the old fashioned style of faculty teaching *to* students (or even *at* them) predominates. Real value comes through the exercise of independent thinking that leads students to analyse, question and challenge.

And also, this is excellent training for the world of business. Managers, especially in top-performing firms, are usually intelligent, argumentative and opinionated. Learning to hold your own in the cut-and-thrust of debate is another essential skill required for personal and professional success.

There are, as a generalization, two kinds of interaction in the active classroom: formal and informal. Formal interaction refers to set-pieces such as lectures and presentations. Informal interaction refers to partly structured or unstructured situations such as question-and-answer sessions and, especially, general discussions.

Presentations

Because the active classroom depends on interaction between the players, students and faculty, there are two aspects to this discussion: how to give presentations, and how to listen to them. We will deal with the former first.

Designing and giving presentations

Presentations are normally given to other students and faculty. They can be simple, as in the presentation of a case write-up, or complex, as some project presentations may be. In most cases, the student will be asked to stay within a certain time limit – for example, presentations should not be more than five minutes long – and may also be advised to use a particular format for the presentation.

It is strongly advised that all presentations, even quite similar ones, should be written out before being delivered in class. Very few of us are confident enough or good enough at rhetoric to be able to deliver an important presentation solely from memory. Some people prefer to speak from fairly simple, point form notes, while others prefer to write their presentations out in full; if you have not done many presentations before and do not know which will be best, experiment and determine which works best for you. Which is most comfortable to deliver, and seems to get your message across best?

If there is a time limit on the presentation, run through it before delivery and time yourself. If the presentation looks like running over length, prune it back (and conversely, if it is too short, consider adding to it; it may be possible to include that important bit of background information which you had earlier discarded). Remember to read or deliver the presentation at the same speed as you will be presenting it live. If you have difficulty with this, try reading the presentation into a tape recorder, then playing it back and timing the tape. This can sometimes be useful for picking out rough spots in the presentation as well.

If you are using illustrated material, rehearse this before the presentation as well. Ensure all slides, exhibits and so on are correct, clear and make sense. Check before going to give the presentation that all these are correct and in the right order. Even the best presenters sometimes get their slides mixed up, and it is not usually a major problem if it happens once. If mixups occur repeatedly, though, this can be distracting for the audience.

In Chapter 6 we discussed some of the principles of written communication, and many of those will apply here. In particular, the AAMR (aims, audience, message, response) model is just as important in oral presentations as in written ones. For oral presentations, consider this model in the following light:

- *aims*: what is the purpose of the presentation? What are its primary ideas, and why should your audience be interested in them?
- *audience*: all presentations have an audience, and how effective they are can only really be measured by their impact on that audience. Who are they, and why are they listening to your presentation? What are they likely to want to take away from it? What level of background knowledge are they likely to have? (In the classroom, answering these questions will be fairly easy; but treat the questions seriously anyway. They will be important in structuring other presentations later.)
- *message*: what message are you trying to get across? How much background information will you need to provide to fill in necessary gaps in what the audience knows? How can your ideas be best expressed? What supporting material (handouts, audio-visual material) would reinforce your case?
- *response*: what response do you want from the audience? Are you asking them questions, or looking to stimulate discussion? If so, pitch your presentation so that they are required to make some response.

As with written presentations too, use a style that is appropriate to the setting. When writing the presentation out beforehand, structure it so that your ideas come in logical order and so that your sentences are easy to follow. Be wary of loading too much information onto the audience too fast. Most people can comprehend information in written form faster than they can orally, so if ideas are really complex, illustrate them with slides, flowcharts, spreadsheets or whatever tools are to hand. Paper handouts to take away and digest later can also be valuable.

Again, though, keep this all in proportion. A complex set of spreadsheets and a five page handout giving background information is appropriate for a serious research project; it isn't for a two-minute presentation of a case write-up. Bigger is not always better.

Above all, be familiar with the material you are presenting. The key to good presenting lies not just in having a stylish presentation, but also in an easy familiarity with the subject which allows the presenter to vary the text, ad libbing if necessary, should the presentation demand it. Ideally, you should know much more than you are going to say. Resist the temptation to pack everything into the presentation itself; slip the extra material in during the discussion afterwards.

How bad can it get?

Everyone who speaks or lectures in public has their horror stories, but fresh in my own memory is the occasion several years ago when, shortly before going in to teach a class of MBA students, my briefcase was stolen from the train on which I was travelling. Needless to say, it contained not only my audio-visual exhibits but also all my own lecture notes. The subject of that day's session was a complex one, which required considerable input from me, and there was no time at all to reconstruct the lecture.

There was no option but to ad lib. I got away with it, because on this occasion I had enough familiarity with the subject that I could recall most of the key points off the top of my head (though not necessarily in which order they should come). Also, I was frank with the audience, explaining the difficulty at the outset, thereby ensuring that their standards of expectation were lowered appropriately (and also that their sympathy was enlisted).

This and any number of other things can go wrong. But in presenting, nearly every problem can be overcome *provided you are familiar with the subject on which you are speaking*. In other words, provided you have enough knowledge, you can innovate your way through problems and difficulties.

And *that* point, of course, applies to many situations besides public speaking.

When standing in front of the class and delivering the presentation, be as natural as you can, but remember to speak clearly and slowly. Vary the pitch of your voice; be emphatic on those points that matter. Especially if reading a presentation, do not read it in a dull flat monotone; speak directly to your audience. Make eye contact with members of the audience occasionally (especially those who do not appear to be paying attention).

If using audio-visual material, remember to refer to this; if you need to turn to point to something on the screen, stand with your back to the audience for as little time as possible. If something goes wrong with the audio-visual presentation, sort it out quickly without getting flustered; if the fault is serious, it is often best to bring the presentation to a halt, and if the fault cannot be quickly fixed, you will need to work from the text as best you can. (Most audiences are quite forgiving in such circumstances; if a similar disaster has not happened to them in the past, it probably will soon.)

Above all, watch the audience. If they look uninterested, change what you are doing; change your stance or the tone of your voice, or turn to the next slide in the presentation. If this doesn't work, consider summarizing quickly what you are saying and get on to the next section of the presentation. (If you cannot rouse them at all, then something has gone wrong; devote some time after the presentation to going through it to find out what. This is valuable learning, at least if it helps you not to make the same mistake twice.)

As with writing, there is really no way to get better at making presentations except by practice. When the opportunity to make presentations comes up, take it if you can. Use the experience to develop your own skills. Plan carefully, and critique your own efforts afterwards. If possible, seek feedback from colleagues and faculty. The standard response from fellow students may well be 'Yeah, yeah, that was fine', regardless of whether the computer froze, the blackboard fell off the wall and you spilled coffee on your notes, but prod them to make sure they are telling the truth. Faculty are usually more impartial (that independence of mind, remember).

Listening to presentations

The same principles of active learning discussed in connection with lectures from faculty apply to presentations by colleagues. Such presentations represent a further source of learning. It is likely that your colleagues will have taken some care over their presentations and are including in them knowledge and ideas of their own, that may be fresh and new to you.

...TENTHLY

Getting involved in the presentation means listening carefully, asking intelligent questions, criticizing where necessary and also giving praise and/or expressing agreement when appropriate. In the discussion or question-and-answer session, each student has the opportunity to analyse and synthesize the information that has been presented, and thus help create further knowledge for the whole group, including themselves.

When engaged in these activities, however, it is important to remember the dignity of those who are speaking. Listen politely and attentively, and give encouragement if the speaker looks like getting stuck. Ask simple, clear questions; be polite, even when criticizing, and be sure to give praise where praise is due. Never be personal in your comments, at least not in class (if you have personal remarks you absolutely must make, save them for a private situation, later). Don't take over the discussion; let others have their turn. Extend to your colleagues the same courtesy you would like extended to you.

Discussions

The same comments apply to general discussions, question-and-answer sessions and so on. I give no rules for these, because there are none; every discussion is unique, its nature wholly dependent on the mix of the subject(s) being discussed and the participants, their views, ideas and knowledge.

The two general principles to be adhered to in such discussions are inclusiveness and respect. Just as in team working (see Chapter 5), try to ensure that the whole group is involved and has something to contribute. This is one of the roles of teaching faculty, of course, but students can assist in this, indirectly by not 'hogging the ball' or attempting to dominate the room, and directly by yielding the floor to colleagues or even asking questions themselves of fellow students who do not appear to be taking part in the discussion. The archetypes we discussed in Chapter 5 are likely to show up here as well, and the same character traits need to be watched for and in some cases compensated for.

Just as with team working, a good general discussion is greater than the sum of its parts in terms of learning and knowledge. Knowledge and ideas are not just passed back and forth, they are actually generated through the processes of analysis and synthesis. Good discussion is one of the best incubators for innovation and creativity. Being able to manage and take part effectively in such a discussion is yet another vitally important communications skill.

The element of respect is also important. Often, people are unnecessarily abrasive or aggressive in classroom situations, seeing this as a way to make their mark on the group and impress faculty. In fact, the quieter person who perhaps makes only half a dozen comments may be more impressive, especially if those comments are particularly perceptive or acute. Adopt the old military principle of 'economy of force': do as much as is needed, but no more. Express your ideas clearly and concisely, but do not overplay your hand. There is no need to ask every question or say out loud every comment that comes to mind (save these for later, when everyone is gathered in the pub talking over the day's events. Bar staff can then be relied on to keep order if fights break out.)

How aggressive is enough?

There is a fine line to be walked here, but I would draw a distinction between *energy* and outright *aggression*. The former refers to being able to get a hearing and put one's views across in a way that means they are understood, and this can at times require some fairly forceful actions and speech. There is nothing wrong with this, so long as the dignity of others is respected. Aggression is when this no longer is the case. Rudeness, interrupting others or talking other people down fall into this latter category. They add little or nothing to the learning experience for the aggressor or for others. They are unlikely to serve one well in a later management career either; most senior managers just *hate* bumptious juniors, and usually find interesting projects for them, like running a seminar on building maintenance and lavatorial cleaning services, or undertaking field work on the market for personal hygiene products in Outer Mongolia.

Far be it from me to tell anyone how to behave, and any reader of this book is free to adopt whatever strategy he or she wishes in group situations, including being aggressive (especially if you like yaks). But there are attendant consequences to such behaviour. A good rule of thumb is: think before you speak.

In general, it is better to work with people rather than against them. Showing respect for others even when you disagree with them usually results in reciprocity. Healthy friendly disagreement can even be a source of creative tension.

Knowledge management

The classroom is, as we have noted above, a place for both acquiring knowledge and using it. Presentations and lectures are valuable sources of knowledge, and careful organization and structuring of any notes, handouts and so on is a good idea if the knowledge obtained is to be maximized. Discussions offer the possibility for using knowledge. Providing inputs from one's own knowledge can help take the discussion forward; other students will be doing the same, and the resulting process of synthesis can result in quite new knowledge being generated and shared among all members of the group.

This process is not unique to the MBA classroom. In many business situations, it is how knowledge actually gets made. Innovation and creativity are sometimes solo efforts, but more often they come out of the work of groups, teams and even entire departments who pass ideas around amongst themselves. (How this process works is described in much more detail by Nonaka and Takeuchi in *The Knowledge-Creating Company* (Oxford: Oxford University Press, 1995).)

Benefit maximization

Use the experience of the classroom to practise these aspects of knowledge management skills. See each presentation or discussion as both an opportunity to learn and an opportunity to contribute to the learning of others. After a while this cast of mind becomes a habit, and you will begin automatically extracting and using knowledge in such a way that the process becomes invisible; knowledge management simply becomes a part of everyday life. If you can achieve this level of thinking, then you are well on the way to success as a manager.

Conclusions

This chapter has looked at how knowledge is transmitted and used in classrooms. Elements of it related directly to Chapter 3 on courses, and also to Chapters 4-6 which look at other aspects of course work. The main thing to remember about the classroom is that it is the focal point of most courses, a crucible in which knowledge is transmitted and generated at a high rate. The classroom *is* an artificial environment, but this does not make it any less valuable. Lectures need not be boring, nor need group discussions be dull. With the right spirit on the part of all parties, each such session can be an opportunity for real learning, and thus a vital part of the MBA experience.

Chapter 8

Research
Generating and creating knowledge

In research, the horizon recedes as we advance.
Mark Pattison

Chapters 3-7 dealt for the most part with courses, which make up the greater part of the MBA experience for most students, and with issues relating to them such as working in teams, classroom interaction, studying and preparing case studies and written communication. The next few chapters look at other topics which are also of importance to MBA students, but which relate to other aspects of the programme.

One such topic is research. The importance of research has been touched on already, for instance when discussing case studies (Chapter 4) when it may be desirable or even necessary to do further background work. Research of this kind is often fairly basic and limited to a relatively small number of sources. Other parts of the programme, such as projects, require more complex research. The management of in-company projects is discussed in more detail in Chapter 9; here, we will look at research in general terms, how it works and how it is best managed.

Research is an important part of knowledge management, one which focuses on acquiring and organizing knowledge (whereas communication, discussed in Chapters 6 and 7, focuses more on organizing and using knowledge). As well as knowledge *acquisition* (obtaining knowledge from another source), we also touch on knowledge *organization*, the storage and management of the acquired knowledge, and knowledge *creation*, as most research necessarily has some creative element.

This chapter concentrates primarily on what is known as 'desk research', or research which concentrates on acquiring information from already published sources, as opposed to 'field research' which involves gathering 'new' data (and is discussed in more detail in Chapter 9). In our definition, close colleagues such as fellow students and faculty are considered under the heading of 'desk research', as they are relatively close to 'home' and getting information from them is not really the same as collecting new data.

One way to look at business schools, as discussed in Chapter 1, is to see them as highly concentrated collections of resources. These resources can be exploited in order to acquire or create knowledge for the individual student. In terms of benefit maximization, knowledge needs to be seen as the other side of communication, the 'input' to communication's 'output'. One cannot speak or write effectively without the benefit of knowledge; at the same time, knowledge which cannot be communicated is ineffective, at least in terms of the needs of modern management. Learning to manage knowledge resources, then, is a necessary complement to learning to manage communication.

The resource-based view of the MBA

Chapter 1 introduced the concept of the 'resource-based' view of the MBA, and suggested that there were four primary sources of knowledge into which students could tap:

- data and information repositories
- faculty
- fellow students
- themselves

There is, however, a fifth source, one which students may need to look into should they be unable to get what they need through the business school. This fifth category, *external resources*, consists of information centres and individuals outside the business school who can be contacted for help when doing research. External resources are usually plentiful but are not always obvious.

Data, information and knowledge

Let us start with a few fundamental concepts first. Chapter 1, when introducing the concept of knowledge management, also noted the existence of a hierarchy of terms, *data*, *information*, *knowledge* and *wisdom* (see Table 1.1). The last of these can be safely left out for the moment, as this is something which is internally generated. Data, information and knowledge, however, can all be the subjects of research.

Data are on the simplest level of the hierarchy. Examples of data which MBA students might run across include:

- economic data for a particular country or market, such as gross domestic product, balance of trade and so on
- financial data, concerning a company, such as the amount of its profit (or loss) in the last financial year
- market data, such as the number of consumers in a market segment, per capita spending on a certain class of product and so on
- production data, such as the number of units a production line is capable of making in a given period of time
- employment data, such as total wage bill, number of employees and so on

These are 'simple' facts or figures which, taken by themselves, mean very little and are capable of many different uses or interpretations. In the example given in Table 1.1, data could be the naturally occurring elements, chemicals, compounds and so on which are found in bread.

Information is on the next most complex level. Examples of data which business school students may find include:

- economic information, whether a particular country or market is booming, is depressed and so on
- financial information, such as a company's performance over time or against expectations
- marketing information, such as the frequency with which consumers buy a particular product, their needs for and expectations of a product, and so on

- production information, such as the efficiency of a production system, its ability to meet quality standards and so on
- employment information, such as the level of training current among employees or factors which might give rise to health and safety problems

Information is usually created by synthesizing different sets of data; for example, financial information is generated by comparing different sets of financial data such as time series, real against planned and so on. In the bread analogy used in Table 1.1, information represents the list of ingredients and the recipe for bread-making, but not the skill to actually make bread.

The laying on of hands

In a television debate in April 2000 on the *Newsnight* programme on BBC2, a businessman attacked a member of the government for increasing the burden of regulation on small firms. Each new tranche of regulations required him, the businessman, to interrupt his work in order to read and study the regulations, to get to know them. Nonsense, replied the man from government. There was no need to study regulations as they came out; they were all available on the Internet.

The fallacy being committed here is interesting. It illustrates the mistaken belief by many people that knowledge has some sort of life of its own, and that to gain knowledge all one has to do is find the source and then absorb the knowledge by osmosis. (In the example above, the man from government presumably thought it was possible to absorb the regulations by logging on to the relevant website and then laying one's hands on the computer screen.) In fact, although it may be possible to get *information* this way, or at least in some similar way, getting knowledge is rather harder work. The businessman would have needed not only to have read and absorbed the *information* in the regulations, he would then have need to develop the *knowledge* of how the regulations would impact on his own business.

Knowledge is more complex still. It is the hardest to learn or teach, since it requires activity by the learner; knowledge cannot simply be passively acquired. In the analogy in Table 1.1, knowledge is the actual skill required to bake bread, the ability to read the recipe, acquire the ingredients and coordinate the process. The list of ingredients (information) is essential, but it is effectively useless without the skill to translate that information into action. Examples of knowledge which MBA students might acquire are discussed throughout this book in the context of the knowledge management system. Essentially, though, whether acquiring background knowledge about a company, market, sector, country, etc. or whether learning a new skill, knowledge requires *the active participation of the person who is learning*. Knowledge cannot be acquired passively.

How this works in practice becomes clear when we look at how research is actually done.

Doing research

The purpose of doing research is to acquire and/or create knowledge. The process itself will probably require looking at all three levels of the hierarchy described above, as each has its own role to play. The process of doing research can be broken down into five components, as follows:

- aims, what is the final intended outcome of the research
- plans, how the research will be carried out and on what timetable
- carrying out the research plan, the actual process of researching
- analysis, the considering of data and information gathered in order to create knowledge
- presentation, the final statement of the research in accordance with the aims

There is not space here to go into a detailed description of research methodologies, and I am not sure such a discussion would be that valuable in any case. Many will have some familiarity with these from undergraduate days or other training programmes, and I also want to avoid getting into any debate about the 'best' way of doing research (maxims like 'start with the facts and work forward' are of only limited use in many business situations; what if there are few verifiable facts, or conversely, what if there is so much data that it is impossible to absorb it all in the time available?). The purpose of this discussion is to suggest some ways for MBA students to design and carry out effective research programmes within very constricted or limited schedules.

Aims

The first step, of course, is to decide what it is you need to know. Try framing this as a question. What is the market potential for widgets in Thailand? What capital investment is likely to be needed by company A's expansion programme in the coming year? Then, when doing this research, try to stick closely to these aims. Use the aims as a standard against which to measure the utility of a potential research source. Can it give you information about the question you have asked? If so, check it out; if not, save your valuable time for other more promising sources.

Nearly all research which MBAs undertake will require some sort of output, either directly in the form of a written paper or report, or indirectly as background knowledge, etc. for another project or a discussion session. Either way, consider the nature of the presentation when establishing your aims. This in turn will help define the scope of the research programme, how many sources must be consulted and so on.

Plans

Having asked the question, the next step is to determine how it will be answered. First, break the question down into its component parts. When answering the question 'what is the market potential for widgets in Thailand', it will usually be necessary to know about widgets themselves, their uses and consumption, and the sectors of the Thai economy/market that might use or consume them. This process will thus give several different sub-categories of knowledge which need to be acquired. The next step is usually to determine what information and knowledge resources exist and where they are located. Can they be accessed easily and quickly and at a reasonable cost? How much information is each source likely to have and how reliable is it? In order to answer the last you will have to either fall back on your own experience or ask someone who is familiar with such sources; faculty and fellow students might both be able to contribute to the answer.

Work out a research strategy, prioritizing the most valuable and most accessible sources. It is usually best when dealing with complex research programmes to set a timetable as well, although this should be flexible. If the research is being carried out by a team (see Chapter 5), assign different classes of sources to different people; thus in the example above, one person would look up the technical information on widgets, while another would gather background information on Thailand, and so on. .

Too much information

Perfect knowledge of a subject requires the consideration of all available information on it. This certainly is the scientific approach, which suggests that we ought not to draw conclusions until we have acquired enough facts to justify them. Sadly, few of us (including many scientists) have the luxury of enough time to carry this theory into practice. We are constantly forced to draw conclusions from insufficient facts, and we make assumptions which help us to paper over the cracks.

This may be lamentable, but it is a fact of life. MBA students will find they never have enough time to research a subject as fully as they would like, and this will carry over into future careers in business. It is best to accept this and design research projects that are realistic in terms of time and availability of sources. Look for maximum utility; get the most data, information and knowledge out of the sources you can reach and examine quickly.

How much information is enough to draw conclusions? There is no hard and fast rule; the answer will depend on the problem, on the nature of the questions you have set yourself. It is for this reason that aims must be defined carefully; if it looks like a research programme is going to be too big to carry out in the time available, consider redefining the question. Similarly, when planning and conducting the research, stay focused on the goals; don't collect information that will not be needed, no matter how much fun or interesting it might look.

For most research projects, including any where a team is involved, the research plan and timetable should be written down and circulated to all members. Any subsequent amendments need to be agreed and incorporated into the written document

Carrying out the research plan

Ways of actually 'doing' research depend to a large extent on the sources being used, and these are discussed in more detail in the following section. Most desk research, however, requires the researcher to sit patiently flipping through pages of material on paper or on screen, making notes. The process is laborious, time-consuming, and often deadly dull. Here are some tips which, if you are not familiar with desk research, might be helpful.

- Don't try to read everything. Develop the ability to 'gut' a document, that is, going through it and quickly pulling out the sections that are relevant to you. Use indexes, word searching facilities and any other tools that will take you to where you want to go. This is not perfect, but it will get you most of the information you need most of the time.
- Always read the introduction first; this alone may tell you whether the document will be relevant at all. If the introduction looks unpromising, too technical or off-topic, consider moving on to another source.
- Make notes of short points, but don't waste time copying or cutting and pasting long passages. Download or photocopy documents which have particular value. Take them away and read them again, highlighting important points.
- Never accept anything you read uncritically. Try to validate data by either ensuring the reliability of the source you are using, or checking against other sources. Solving a problem using the wrong data almost invariably leads to the wrong answer.
- Try to form a judgement as you read as to what is the author's opinion and what can be verified as (relatively) factual. Look at the sources he/she/they are using and consider looking at some of these yourself if there is time.

How the author interprets a source and how you interpret it
might be quite different.

Analysis

This is a critical stage in any research, since at this point you are
not so much getting data, information or knowledge as looking
at what you have acquired and trying to decide on its meaning,
worth or value. This is difficult, because in order to do this you
already have to have some background knowledge; otherwise
you would not be able to form a judgement at all. If, for example,
you have zero knowledge of accounting and financial management, a profit and loss account is just a meaningless jumble of
figures. On the other hand, *some* of what lies behind the material
you have gathered is likely to always be hidden. For example,
even if you were fully expert in all aspects of accounting and
financial management, the accounts of a particular company
would still require some explanation, unless you were fully
familiar with that company and all its circumstances (and maybe
not even then).

To make sense of the material that has been researched, then,
it is necessary to apply one's own mind and knowledge to the
material itself and then ask two questions:

- How sensible is it?
- How likely is it to be correct?

This is not a case of the same question being asked in two
different ways. It is quite possible in business for something to
seem sensible and yet turn out to be wrong. Some (possibly
apocryphal) research from the USA claims that 58 per cent of all
managerial decisions are wrong, but to the people who made
those wrong decisions, at the time they undoubtedly made
sense.

To answer the first question, it is necessary to apply logic,
common sense, intuition or any mixture of the three you care to
use. Consider whether any given statement or piece of
information seems sensible in its context. If a market intelligence report suggests there is a likely market for widgets in

Thailand, this may well seem sensible, if the other material you have gathered confirms this. If you have other statements or material casting doubt on the statement of the widget market, though, then you are justified in questioning the first author's wisdom.

Determining the likelihood of a statement's being correct can be dealt with through analysis and verification. Verification, or checking whether statements are true, is usually best done by checking other authorities on the same subject and seeing whether they bear one another out (but be careful of groupthink; check the sources of these authorities and make sure they are not just quoting one another). In ideal conditions one might wish to replicate the research done by the original authority in reaching his/her/their conclusions, but time and resources seldom allow this.

Where information cannot be verified, its likelihood of truth can be determined through analysis or *critical reasoning*. Anne Thomson, in *Critical Reasoning: A Practical Introduction* (London: Routledge, 1995) gives a checklist for applying critical reasoning to the conclusions offered by authorities, which is reproduced (with some minor amendments) below.

1   Find the conclusion.
2   Find the reasons the authority gives for this conclusion, and work out any unstated assumptions which the authority is making.
3   Consider how far you can go in assessing the truth of the reasons and the unstated assumptions. Think about how you would seek further information to enable you to assess the truth of the reasons.
4   Does the reasoning rely on evidence from sources whose authority is questionable?
5   Do you yourself have any knowledge which strengthens or weakens the conclusion? (Remember to subject your own knowledge to the same standards of scrutiny as you apply to claims made by other people.)
6   Does the passage contain any explanations? If so, are they plausible and are they the only plausible explanations of what is being explained?

7   If you believe that the conclusion is not well supported by the reasons and assumptions, can you state the way in which the move from reasons to conclusions is flawed?
                (*Critical Reasoning: A Practical Introduction*, p. 61)

This list is a good tool for examining arguments and for demolishing those which do not ultimately stand up. Thomson gives a quick example, of a scientist who 'proved' that the Loch Ness monster could not possibly exist because the fish stocks in Loch Ness were too small to support a beast of such size. A letter to the *Independent* newspaper used critical reasoning to dispose of this 'proof'; it was equally possible, the writer argued, that there were few fish in Loch Ness because the monster had eaten them all!

And that brings up another point; logic and analysis can be used to prop up bad arguments, and to demolish good ones, if used improperly. Ultimately, submit everything to the test of common sense.

Presentation

Chapter 6 dealt with written presentations in detail, and Chapter 7 also discussed oral presentations in the classroom; the same comments will apply to most presentations made in other environments. When presenting research, the most important thing is to answer fully and clearly, with appropriate levels of supporting information and data, the question that was asked in the 'aims' stage, above. That is what the presentation should do, and that is all it should do. Reams of absolutely fascinating supporting information may have been gathered and a great deal of knowledge acquired along the way. In the presentation, though, select what is appropriate; store the rest for later use (give some handouts showing important points if you absolutely must, but use even this tool sparingly).

Using information and knowledge resources

Once the student knows how to design and manage a research programme, using the classes of resource mentioned at the start of this chapter becomes comparatively simple. Each category has its strengths, and also its weaknesses.

NON COMPUTERISED VISUAL LEARNING RESOURCE

Data and information repositories

These are the first tool of the desk researcher, and it is from these that nearly all data and information will be gleaned. CD-ROMs and the Internet have made a great impact in this area, but the good old-fashioned book continues to have its uses.

Books

Books continue to be the places to go for what I call 'considered knowledge'; detailed expositions, long views, considered opinions. The academic system is structured so that most faculty ultimately aim to produce their major work in book form. Books are thus very valuable if you need background information, but they are also detailed expositions of the knowledge of experts on particular topics. Their major drawbacks tend to be complexity (they can take a long time to read, especially if there is no proper index or contents list) and datedness (time to press requirements mean every book is at least several months out of date by the time it appears in print, and most are rather more than that).

Journals

Journals proliferate in management and business, and no matter what subject you are trying to research, there is probably at least one journal that covers it. The problem with journals is finding the material. Fortunately, CD-ROM and online indexes are now available which allow topic and name searches, and this simplifies things greatly. Then, many journals have very small circulations, and the journal you want may not be available in your library, or in any library nearby. Familiarity will also tell you which journals are useful for which purposes; some are very technical, others are very focused on hands-on management, still others appear to have no discernable purpose. These are a valuable specialist resource, but can be time-consuming to use.

Electronic and on-line information

The two major problems with this type of resource are volume and quality control. Search engines are getting better (gone are the days when anyone searching for information on 'China' would get several hundred sites concerning Royal Doulton and Wedgwood as well as the People's Republic of China), but one can still spend a long time trying to find the one useful website in the list of ten thousand or so that the search throws up. If you have not already done so, spend some time using search engines and getting familiar with them, learning the techniques that will allow you to refine your searches in the shortest possible time.

As anyone can post anything on the World Wide Web, there is absolutely no guarantee of the information's quality or truth. The only defence is to apply rigorously methods of analysis and verification. Some information is published electronically by reliable sources; a lot isn't. There is a lot of potentially valuable material out there, but it is up to you to determine what is gold and what is iron pyrites (fool's gold).

Faculty

Data and information come primarily from repositories, but knowledge is likely to come in large part from teaching faculty. It is not usually a good idea to use them for sources of data; citing the gross domestic product of Bolivia on the basis of a figure given you by a member of faculty is unlikely to be acceptable in a final report (i.e., you should go and look it up yourself). The real role of faculty as a resource comes in providing knowledge and opinions which can be used to analyse and verify material already gathered. Does something appear not to make sense? Talk it over with an expert. Perhaps he or she can set your mind at rest, or perhaps will confirm your view. Either way, you can take the next step in your analysis.

Faculty also are useful as guides to information and data sources. If you are stuck for ideas about what to read next, try approaching a member of faculty whose interests accord with the topic being researched. The chances are they will be able to direct you to a source, or at least provide some leads.

Fellow students

Colleagues on the programme are likely to have less specialist knowledge than faculty, but they will have valuable views and ideas to input nonetheless. Use them to check the results of your analysis and ideas. Do your own interpretations of the facts stand up? Are your conclusions logical? Is there anything you have missed? Also, most of your colleagues will also be involved in research of their own, in different fields. If you are running out of sources, ask around if anyone knows where to find information on your subject. If your network is good enough, the chances are someone will have run across a similar source and be able to direct you to it.

Yourself

I have belaboured this point already, so I will be brief. Gathering information requires few special skills or abilities; anyone with the right training can do it. Gathering *knowledge* is rather different; it is a proactive process which requires you to actively go out and seek knowledge. It follows from this that in the research process, you yourself are a resource. Your cognitive abilities and previous knowledge are the critical tools in the research process. If one or both is not functioning as it should, then the task will become more difficult.

Organize and store knowledge already acquired so it is ready for use in future research projects, to help analyse and verify new material. Practise the techniques of critical reasoning; make yourself familiar with the basics of logic, if you are not already so; and above all, apply common sense. With these abilities, it is possible to manage most research programmes.

External resources

External resources are libraries, data centres, companies, experts and other people located outside the business school, and who cannot be reached directly from within the school (as, say, websites can). Using external resources is pretty much like using the categories above. The real trick is in finding them and getting access to them.

One early step in the MBA programme is to find out what other institutions will allow you library access, and make sure you are registered with these. (You can never, in my view, have too many library passes.) If you know a piece of information you want is in a certain library but do not have access, try using whatever influence you have through your business school to get in. Most government and corporate libraries will, if approached often enough, grant temporary passes.

Getting hold of people is another matter. You can try simply calling direct and making an appointment to go and see the person you want, and you might succeed. If you fail, again use the influence of the school. Ask your faculty supervisor or tutor if the school has any contacts with the person or their organization. In other words, use the network.

Using external resources can be time-consuming and frustrating, but it is good practice. When you ultimately leave the business school and return to the world of business, many of the resources the business school offers will be left behind; you will need to discover, or rediscover, your own sources, and most of these will be external to your own organization.

Knowledge management

As this chapter has described, research is a key part of knowledge management. It is a primary process through which knowledge is directly acquired and then organized and stored, ready for use. At the same time, the research process also requires the use of prior knowledge when analysing the quality of newly acquired knowledge. Research is thus part of a cycle of knowledge acquisition and use which, if kept in motion, results in a process of continuous learning. This is a pre-requisite in modern management for such vital concepts as creativity and innovation.

Benefit maximization

Accordingly, developing research skills is an important part of the MBA experience. As with other skills, use the opportunities presented by research projects to not only complete the project but also develop the skills being used. Analyse your own performance during and after the project. Is the research being carried out effectively? Did you manage your time in the best

relations, and field research. The chapter concludes by looking at three particular aspects of projects which make them valuable: the sense of realism, the opportunity to add real value for the client, and the opportunity to network and make contacts.

What makes a good project?

When setting up an in-company project, it is important not to take on too much. Time for completion will be limited, and so in all probability will be available resources. Work closely with both the client and the business school when establishing and setting up the project to make sure that the project will make a contribution and add value, but also that it is realistic in scope.

A community of interest joins all the parties here: the students doing the project, the managers and company sponsoring it, the business school that has links with both. When working on a project, it is always necessary to keep these other parties and their interests in mind.

A good project is one that leaves a satisfied client. Creating a favourable impression, making new contacts to add to one's network, and perhaps even a job offer, can all be outcomes. A bad project, on the other hand, leaves the client disillusioned and dissatisfied, not only with those who carried out the project but perhaps with MBA students more generally.

The chapter thus covers the following subjects:

- identifying a project
- establishing the aims of a project
- developing relationships with the client
- setting up a research programme
- carrying out field research
- analysis of data gathered
- written and oral presentation
- following up the project with the client

Identifying a project

The first stage is, of course, to identify a suitable project. How this happens will vary between business schools. Some have lists of projects which have been supplied to the school by corporate contacts, and the school then plays a role in matching students with projects. Others encourage students to go out, make contacts and identify their own projects; still others use a combination of methods, encouraging entrepreneurship but providing lists of previously identified projects to those who need them.

Regardless of the method, the initial identification of a project will usually be in fairly vague terms. That is, there will be a topic of mutual interest, but without clearly defined aims. Most projects come about as a result of a company's 'need to know more' about a given subject. These topics can be very diverse, ranging from technology to markets, employees to customers, strategy to operations.

By the time it becomes necessary to identify a project, most students should be well along the MBA programme, and a clearer picture will be emerging of their interests and knowledge needs. Where possible, try to identify a project which fits in with your own goals. Projects offer the opportunity for practical experience and contacts in fields or sectors in which you may already have an interest. If you wish to pursue a career in corporate finance, look for a project which has finance-based issues at its heart.

This may seem odd, given that I have earlier argued for a greater breadth and depth of learning and for using the MBA to gain new experiences and knowledge in new fields. But there are pragmatic issues here. Recruiting companies are often keenly interested in project experience, and will probably ask questions about it. If, as in the example above, you are interested in a career in corporate finance but do a project on marketing fast-moving consumer goods, you will need to be able to show the experience of the latter was relevant to your expectations of the former. What did you learn from the project that would help you in corporate finance?

If you think that on the conclusions of the project you can demonstrate such value, well and good; go ahead and do it. If you cannot, then think again. There are other ways of adding extra value, of course. Choosing a corporate finance project but one which focuses on an unusual area or region (banking in Brazil, say) can be a way of doing so; just remember that there might not be sufficient time or resources to actually go to Brazil to do field work. In the end, we come back to the basic principle: pick a project with care, one that is feasible in the time allowed and one which adds value to the MBA experience and your career.

Project teams

Unlike most management situations, where a project is identified and a team is assembled to deal with it, in most MBA projects the team is assembled first and then picks a project. This can lead to difficulties in project identification if team members have very diverse goals. When putting together a project team, then, it is best to try to pick members who are broadly focused on the same kinds of goals.

Broadly: but not entirely. There is value too in having a diversity of backgrounds, especially as some projects will require a cross-functional approach. The need, then, is to ensure sufficient diversity to provide a range of skills and background knowledge, but also a similarity of interests so that team members are not in conflict and can all derive benefit from the the project.

Part-time and Executive MBA students may have a bit more leeway in this matter. It will be difficult, unless several students on the same programme are working for the same company, to put together a standard student team. The options then are twofold: to work alone, or to put together an in-company team with the student as one member. The former may be necessary, but is probably the second best option. The latter should be possible; if the company believes in the need for the project, then it should be possible to convince them also to free up some management time for it.

Establishing aims

Once the project team are together and a suitable project has been identified, the team should begin working to narrow down the topic and establish the exact aim of the project. As noted in Chapter 8, this can be done by stating the end goal of the project as the answer to a question. For example, what will be the impact of the introduction of a new technology?

However, unlike the kinds of research projects described in Chapter 8, where the researchers are free to decide on their own

WASN'T THAT THE YEAR OF THE STUDENT EFFICIENCY PROJECT?

aims, in in-company projects the aims must ultimately be decided by the client. Essentially, the student teams are acting as consultants to the company, their client. What the client wants is what matters; whether the project is ultimately defined as a success will depend on whether the client company is satisfied.

Developing relationships with the client

Accordingly, one of the first steps in a successful project is to develop relationships with the client. Spend some time with your contact managers; build up a general picture of the situation. Do some background reading on the company in general. Try putting yourself in the position of the client and understanding the pressures they may be facing and the targets they are trying to meet. Then try to direct the project so that it fits in with this bigger picture.

Initially, there may be a need for some negotiation. What the client initially asks for may be more than the team can give, depending on their time and other commitments. An important concept at this point is *managing expectations*. Be careful not to promise anything which the team cannot do, or may not be able to do in the time allowed. Make sure the client is clear as to what his or her company will get at the end of the project. At the same time, be positive about the value the team can deliver.

Many in-company projects offer some sort of fee to the student team. If this is the case, it is well to have a contract or letter of agreement, as in any other form of consultancy. Check with your business school on this point; student teams should always have a member of faculty as a supervisor, who should be able to answer questions on this issue.

As well as the aims of the project, the team and client should also agree on a schedule for the work. The most important date is the delivery of the final report, but intermediate stages should be agreed as well. Schedule any necessary meetings well in advance, as the client managers are likely to be busy and this project will be just one of their many priorities.

Above all, be fair and honest in dealings with the client. If the schedule looks like slipping, let them know, giving reasons (but not excuses); at the same time, give them a realistic revised schedule. If some part of the project cannot be completed in the time allowed, because of lack of resources or other problems that have arisen, again, let the client know. Try to offer them some additional benefit in exchange if possible, but above all, be straightforward with them. Some consultants are of course anything but straightforward with clients, but these consultants don't tend to get repeat business.

The in-company report is a service, which your team is providing to the client and which in many cases they are paying for. It is up to them to define needs; it is up to your team to manage expectations and ensure delivery. These goals can best be achieved by maintaining good relations with the client, to make sure that information about the project is always available to them. You are in effect selling your skills and talents; possibly not for the first time, and most definitely not for the last time in your career in management. Again, this experience should be made to count.

Setting up the research programme

Chapter 8 talked about the process of setting up a research programme, and most of the same principles apply here. The first stage, once the programme's aims have been agreed, is to plan how the research will be carried out and to set a timetable.

The first step is to go back to the aims, and look at the kinds of knowledge which are going to be required. Break the acquisition of these down into separate tasks. If desk research is going to be required on several subjects, treat the research on each subject as a separate task. If field work is needed, break this down as well into separate tasks such as designing the questionnaire or interview questions, carrying out the work, tabulating the results and so on.

If research is required (and it almost always is), follow the steps given in Chapter 8 to determine likely sources of information. In in-company projects, resources external to the business school will almost always be required. Prominent among these, of course, will be the client company's own records and documents and members of its management team. In other words, you will need to tap into the company's own store of knowledge in order to answer the question they have asked you.

Why us?

At some point in most consultancy projects, someone on the team asks, 'Why are they getting us to do this? They could easily have done it themselves.'

Outsiders are brought in for several reasons. The most important are as follows:

- the company may have much of the knowledge and skills it needs to solve a problem, but not all of them. Outsiders are brought in to add missing pieces to the puzzle.
- the company may not be aware just how much knowledge it already has and where. In other words, its own knowledge management systems may be deficient.
- the company's managers may simply lack the confidence to solve their own problems and feel more comfortable relying on an outside expert.
- the company may lack the internal resources needed to put all the pieces together, and be relying on the consultants to carry out this task for it.

Bear this in mind as you are dealing with the client, and try to work out the company's motivations for bringing you in. Often the answer is a combination of several of the above.

Among other tasks, assign someone the responsibility of taking notes of meetings and circulating these to other members of the team, on paper or by e-mail. Someone should also have prime responsibility for client contact, and be the first phone number or e-mail address which the client can contact if need be. (If the contact person is away for any length of time, advise the client and give a substitute address for the period of absence.)

Once a list of necessary tasks has been compiled, prioritize and determine the order in which they should be carried out. If working in a team, of course several tasks can be carried out simultaneously, with one or more team members looking after each. This is by far the best approach; doing tasks in strict order one after another is more time-consuming and generally less satisfying.

Then begin sharing the tasks out among group members. Try to apportion these according to the group's own talents, background knowledge and experience, and interests. Ensure an even division of labour if possible. Project work is *learning by doing*, and members of the team who do not fully take part will have fewer chances for learning (see also Chapter 5). All this – what the tasks are, the order in which they are to be carried out and by whom – should be written down and every member of the team should have a copy. If clients show an interest in the research plan, give them a copy too.

By now the team should know what they need to do, when and in what order, and who will be doing the work. The ultimate aim of the plan is to answer the question posed in the project aims. The next stage is to do the research.

Carrying out field research

Chapter 8 discussed desk research in relation to in-school projects, but its principles can be applied to desk research for in-company projects as well. In addition to desk research, though, in-company projects may require *field research*, or research which aims to generate quite new data. Field research is generally more difficult and more problematic than desk research, and doing it is a skill in its own right.

There are three general sources of information on field research for business school students:

- courses: some schools have elective courses on research methods, and a few even include it as part of the core curriculum
- faculty: supervising faculty will be experienced at field research and can give advice on setting up a research programme
- textbooks: most business school libraries will contain books on research methods, though some of these may be too complex for what your team requires

All three should be considered, although the first option may not be practical or possible and the third, as mentioned, may be too technical. Faculty, though, should always be consulted on the best ways of setting up a research programme.

Keep it simple, stupid

My own rule of thumb for designing field research programmes is the KISS (Keep it Simple, Stupid) rule. Field research is time-consuming and hard work, both to collect and to analyse. Properly done, it generates invaluable data; get it wrong, and you have a mess that can be impossible to sort out. The most common mistake in field research at the MBA level is to do too much.

In the first place, don't even attempt field research unless you have to! There are only two real reasons for doing field research: (1) there is no available data, or (2) there is data available, but it is perceived as being unreliable. (Actually there is another reason: (3) the client expects it. If you don't believe that (1) or (2) are the case, try gently and circumspectly to talk them out of it; but there may be no way around this one.)

Second, if you are committed to field research, don't overdo it; don't design a questionnaire or an interview that will collect masses of information that is only vaguely relevant to the research in question. Get the data you need and get out. Remember the military principle we mentioned in the previous chapter: *economy of force*.

Another general rule to follow when doing field research is to ensure a professional approach. Make sure questionnaires are neatly presented and easy to read. Adopt a professional demeanour when doing interviews; you may be 'only' an MBA student, but you are also a consultant doing an important job. Phone ahead to make arrangements for meetings and interviews. Be punctual. In other words, treat your subjects as you yourself would like to be treated were you in their shoes.

For reasons of space, we will deal here with just two kinds of field research: *questionnaires* and *interviews*.

Questionnaires

Questionnaires are ideally used when a fairly large group of people are to be surveyed, but where the amount of data required from each is fairly small. They can be administered in two ways. The first method is *assisted*, where the survey administrators and the people being surveyed complete the questionnaire together;

the annoying people who stop you in the street and ask you about your favourite films or where you take your holidays are doing assisted questionnaires. The other method is *unassisted*, in which the questionnaire is sent to the people being surveyed by post or e-mail, and the latter are asked to complete the form and send it back. The annoying forms that your insurance company or your car dealership sometimes send you are unassisted questionnaires.

The word 'annoying' is used deliberately, because most people *hate* questionnaires. Most recipients do what most of us do; on receipt of a questionnaire, we ignore it. Market researchers reckon that a 30 per cent response rate to a questionnaire is very good indeed.

When designing a questionnaire, keep the following points in mind:

- most of the people you send the questionnaire to will probably not answer (unless directly ordered to do so by a senior manager, and probably not even then), so make sure your sample size – the number of people to whom the questionnaire is sent – is big enough to allow a reasonable amount of data to come back.
- the questionnaire should be as short as possible; one side of a sheet of paper if possible, and two at most. Telephone questionnaires should take no more than five minutes to go through. Shorter questionnaires are more likely to be answered than are long ones.
- make responding to the questionnaire as easy as possible. If sending it by post, include return postage. If administering an assisted questionnaire by telephone, never cold-call a manager who is to be surveyed; write or e-mail beforehand and arrange a time when they can be at the phone. Let them know in advance how long it will all take.
- remember that the more questions you ask, the more data you will have to compile afterwards. Ask yourself again whether the data you are seeking are all strictly necessary. Pare the questionnaire down as much as you can.

These are general rules which need to be observed when formulating *any* questionnaire. There are many other rules concerning sampling, control groups, statistical significance and so on which we will not go into here; consult an expert (usually a member of faculty) about how to observe and deal with these. These are the sorts of rules you need to follow to ensure the results of the questionnaire are valid and properly analysed. The rules I have given above are ones you need to follow to get the questionnaire answered in the first place; which, in most daily management situations, is a lot more important.

Interviews

Interviews are longer and more complex, and are best used when the number of people to be surveyed is quite small but where relatively large amounts of data are required. Interview techniques follow two types. *Structured interviews* are ones where the interviewer follows a set lists of questions and records the answers given. Basically, these are a form of extended questionnaire. *Unstructured interviews* are ones where the interviewer sets a topic but lets the interviewee describe it in his or her own words.

Both types have their uses. Structured interviews are preferred where the interviewee is required to give views on a fairly broad range of topics. Should the research programme require interviews with twenty managers about the operation of European financial markets in general, a structured interview will almost certainly be required; in an unstructured situation, the twenty will almost certainly talk on vastly different subjects and it will be difficult to obtain comparable data. Structured interviews generate more uniform results and, if the questions are properly designed, generate less unusable data. However, they can lack flexibility.

Unstructured interviews work best when the sample are describing a fairly specific idea, concept or event. They work well, for example, in the research method known as *critical incident technique*, where a number of people who have been involved in an event (such as the delivery of service to a client) are asked to describe the event from their own perspective. They generate masses of data in the form of both facts and opinions, and require some sifting to get at the data that are wanted. They are, however, easier to administer than structured interviews; in most cases, a few questions will suffice to get the interviewee going, and only a few more are needed to keep them on topic. Let's face it: most managers *love* to talk about themselves and their work. Their colleagues, spouses, children and pets have all heard their stories a hundred times and refuse to listen any longer. Any interviewer who ventures within range is likely to be made warmly welcome.

Like questionnaires, interviews need a finite length. An hour is usually enough for most people; half an hour is better still. Work out how long you expect the interview to be, and inform the interviewee of this when first making the appointment to see them; this is helpful as it allows them plan their own schedules.

Analysis of data gathered

When all the required data, information and knowledge have been gathered, then comes the most critical process: analysing and producing a result. Chapter 8 discussed analysis, and little needs to be added beyond a reminder to keep focused on the aims of the project. Don't answer questions that have not been asked (unless you are convinced that they *should* have been asked and are of vital importance).

As with in-school research, go over the material you have gathered and analyse it closely. Consider going back and doing supplementary research if gaps appear in your knowledge. If you must make assumptions at this stage, present these clearly as such, with your reasoning plain behind them. Make sure all the data and information which support your conclusion can be validated. Examine your own reasoning, using the techniques of critical reasoning, for possible flaws. Test every conclusions you reach; if you don't spot the weaknesses, the client will.

Presentation

Finally comes the stage of presenting the results of the work to the client. Most clients will ask for both a written report, which can be circulated, and an oral presentation to the relevant managers. If they ask for a written report only, volunteer to give a presentation as well; it is good practice.

As above, standards of professionalism need to apply. By now, the members of the team will already have gained much experience of writing reports and presenting presentations, and if, as suggested in Chapters 6 and 7, they have been using this experience to develop their own skills, they will be more confident and capable of presenting 'for real'. Written reports need to be clear and well-presented. Oral presentations likewise need to be polished; do at least one 'dress rehearsal' of the full presentation before giving it to the client, and work out the kinks. If a team is presenting, work out clearly who will do what during the presentation; try to make sure everyone has a chance to speak and be heard, but make sure the transition between speakers is smooth and does not distract the audience.

Following up

After the presentation has been given and/or the written report circulated, give the client company time to digest the results. Then contact the client again, by telephone, letter or in person as seems most appropriate. You do not have to do this; it will probably not be expected, and you will almost certainly not get marks or grades for doing so. But it is good professional practice, and it will be appreciated.

Follow-ups need not be formal, but they should do the following:

- ask if the client has had a chance to look at the full report, and if so, if the company has any comments.
- ask is there any area of the report which the client found unsatisfactory.
- ask what parts of the report the client found most valuable, and what if any value it has added for the company.
- ask if the client has given any thought to whether any aspects of the report will be implemented.

Following up can be valuable in helping to determine whether the client was satisfied with the report, and also in determining what if anything went wrong; it can thus be a very useful aspect of learning. Also, it will help to make the client feel good. A follow-up call or visit will help the client to think that you care about them and are committed to their company's well-being, even though perhaps, strictly speaking, you no longer are. It might even help stimulate them to act on your report, by reminding them of its good points.

Knowledge management and projects

In-company projects require the full range of knowledge management:

- knowledge acquisition is required to work out the background to the problem and acquire supporting information and data, including through field research;
- knowledge organization is essential to manage this flow of data and information and make sure it is used properly when analysing the problem and formulating solutions;
- knowledge use is required when analysing the problem, deciding on the solution and presenting this to the client. More, the team is also involved here in *creating* new knowledge which is then passed on to the client.

As such, in-company projects require a synthesis of the various individual knowledge management skills the student has been acquiring in earlier stages of the MBA programme, particularly those relating to research, analysis and communication.

In the medieval and early modern periods, a craftsman could only graduate from journeyman status to that of master by creating a special work, one which both summed up and showed off the full range of the craftsman's skills. The MBA project is a little like that, in that (ideally, at least) it requires the team to use to the full the skills they have learned on the programme. Seeing projects as a masterclass in knowledge management is probably quite a good way of approaching them.

Benefit maximization

There are a whole range of benefits to be gained from a successful project. Enhanced knowledge management skills is one; the experience of doing a project should improve these still further. But there are three others which should also accrue, and which are in some ways unique to this part of the programme: real experience, the opportunity to innovate and add value, and the chance to network.

Working 'under fire'

One of the most valuable aspects of in-company projects is of course the sense of realism. This is not an exercise. There is more at stake here than just marks and grades. If you make mistakes on a project and the client spots them, they will devalue you accordingly (and as, at the end of the MBA programme, some recruiters check references with companies for which students did projects, this can have serious consequences). If the company fails to spot your mistakes but acts on the report, the consequences can be be even more serious.

Projects should not be treated in the same way as classroom work. You will be working with professionals, and you will be expected to be professional. And professionalism is not just a way of behaving around other people; it is a state of mind.

By the point in an MBA programme where you begin to do a project, you should already be well advanced in the learning experience. You will have worked on your skills in terms of both research and communication, and you will have experience of managing team work and organizing for effective knowledge management. The in-company project puts these skills to the test in a real-life situation, with real consequences for failure but also real rewards for success.

Adding value for the client

One of those rewards is the chance to add value for the client. In other words, the success of the project could make a real difference to the company that sponsors it, in terms of improving communication, making production more efficient, developing better systems for managing people, selling more product and so on. Even if the report does not have this *direct* effect in and of itself, it can still make a valuable contribution to such improvements.

A good report answers the questions a client has asked, and therefore creates satisfaction. A very good report does something more. Marketers often speak of two terms, *customer satisfaction* and *customer delight*. The former is when customers' needs and expectations have been met; they have got exactly what they wanted. The latter occurs when needs and expectations have been *exceeded* and customers get even more value than they had asked for.

Though the aim of the project is to create customer satisfaction, be on the lookout for opportunities to create customer delight. If you can find some aspect of the problem the client had not considered, develop this more fully. If you have a suggestion for changes or innovations that would exceed the targets the client has set, consider bringing it into the report. Do this in consultation with the client beforehand, though; at all costs, resist the temptation to 'surprise' them in the final report or presentation. Few managers like bombshells, even friendly ones.

If no such opportunities come up, do not be disappointed; not every client-customer relationship has the potential for customer delight. Customer satisfaction is a valuable goal in its own right, and should be sought for in the first instance. The point about customer delight is that it requires innovative thinking; and this means not only being able to spot opportunities when they exist, but also being able to see clearly when opportunities do *not* exist.

Opportunities for networking

Finally, in-company projects are terrific opportunities for expanding your network of contacts, especially if you have managed to get a project close to your own areas of interest. It is not unknown for satisfied clients to offer jobs to members of successful project teams. Even if they do not, the people you meet and make contact with in the course of the project can become valuable members of your personal network. Networking is discussed more fully in the chapter that follows.

Conclusions

The in-company project is rightly regarded as one of the most valuable aspects of most MBA programmes. It provides valuable practical experience, it is a chance to use and improve a full range of skills, and it offers opportunities for networking with professionals.

The project should be treated with due seriousness, and approached and carried out in a fully professional manner. There is a temptation, though, to see the project as separate from the rest of the programme, because it is 'real' and other aspects such as classroom learning are not. But many of these other activities play a valuable supporting role in project work. Without the knowledge gained from classroom work, for example, carrying out a project successfully would be much more difficult as the necessary skills would not be there. If this were not the case, MBA programmes could simply skip all the boring lectures and case studies and send students out to do projects. (Some argue that this what they should do in any case; wrongly, in my opinion).

Instead of separating the two, see them as a continuous process. The course work earlier in the programme helps build up both background knowledge, management skills, and above all the ability to manage knowledge. The project is an opportunity to practise all these and see learning put to work. There is no conflict here; instead, both course work and projects are simply different parts of the whole MBA experience.

Chapter 10

Networking
Creating value out of harmony

A man must make his opportunity, as oft as find it.
Sir Francis Bacon

Networking has an odd reputation among managers, particularly those from Anglo-Saxon countries like Britain and the USA. Views on the subject fall into two camps. On the one hand there are many, including very senior and otherwise successful people, who find networking very difficult to do: they are uneasy when attempting to network, and may even regard networking by others with suspicion. Others regard networking as a natural part of both professional and personal life, and cannot see what all the fuss is about. This is also true of many managers from cultures such as Japan and especially China, where networking is natural and commonplace.

Between these two groups there is little middle ground, and one consequence is that there are few people able to sit down and think objectively about what networking *is* and what activities constitute it. There are many formal or quasi-formal attempts to teach networking, and I have a special word for these which I will introduce later in this chapter. But what most Western managers need is a model for networking which they can use in their daily lives.

In fact, networking is one of the most important benefits which the MBA programme provides. Graduates should ideally leave the programme with both the beginnings of a network (or alternatively, valuable additions to pre-existing networks) and, perhaps more critically, with an enhanced ability to network. The reason for this is simple: the structure of most MBA programmes means that students *must* work together and perforce get to know one another. There is, therefore, an opportunity to use the MBA experience to develop networking abilities.

Is networking a skill?

Some people attempt to teach networking as if it were a skill, with clearly defined tools and methods which, if employed properly, will lead to the creation of successful networks. I am not altogether convinced of this, any more than I am that raising children requires 'parenting skills'. There *are* some useful tools which can be used for networking, but they tend to be simple things like diaries and address books. The most important assets in creating a good network are things like personality, respect for others (and self-respect), professionalism and knowledge and understanding of other people's feelings. Part psychology, part intuition, good networking is more of an attitude of mind; a philosophy, even.

Some of the skills discussed already in this book *are* important in networking though, especially communication skills. So networking may not be *a* skill, but it does require *skills*.

The purpose of this chapter is to explain and clarify the nature of networking and to show how it functions within the confines of the MBA experience. Some important issues are considered, including ethical standards in networking. Networking is then considered in three related areas: formal situations in the MBA programme, informal situations in the MBA programme, and after the programme has finished.

Networks and their benefits

The advantages of a good network of business contacts are numerous. Just a few of them are stated here:

- exchanging news and information; a good network allows you to gather news and hear information, sometimes before rivals or competitors do.

- knowledge resources; when acquiring new knowledge, your contacts can be an important additional source on whom you can draw formally or informally.
- professional assistance and advice; this kind of professional support can be valuable at almost any time.
- personal support; often important when undertaking big steps such as changing jobs, relocation or overseas placements.
- support for career advancement; friends and colleagues in your network can for example advise on new job or promotion opportunites.

The ability to network is being seen as a critical attribute in a manager by many companies today, and success in many jobs is often contingent on a manager's ability to make his or her networks perform.

Terms

Networking is often used synonymously with other terms, such as relationship building, relationship management and network management. All are basically the same, though defnitions may vary in detail (depending on who you ask). Networking, the older term, is preferred here, but feel free to substitute the term or word of your choice.

A good network has two aspects: *breadth* and *depth*. A broad network includes a lot of different people, in different professions and walks of life, from different educational and cultural backgrounds, and possessing different kinds and degrees of knowledge. How *deep* a network is refers to the intensity of the relationships between members, and this in turn reflects on how often and to what extent members can call on one another. It is quite possible to be a member of several different networks – indeed, most of us are – and some of these will be broader and deeper than others.

Networks are important for exactly the same reason that teams are: they extend the scope and reach of each individual in the network. A manager who is part of a good functioning network will have access to much more, and probably much better, information and knowledge than one who works in isolation. Who has better knowledge: the manager who has a long lunch every day, or the one who stays in and works through lunch? A good question; in fact, both probably have access to equal quantities of knowledge, but the luncher's will be more diverse, come from different sources and perhaps be subjected to more scrutiny and analysis (especially once the party is onto the second bottle of wine).

There is a further point to consider: organizations themselves are basically networks, with horizontal and vertical lines of communication connecting individuals, teams and departments. Business organizations function by coordinating the activities of their members. It follows that if you understand networking, you are enhancing your skills and abilities as a manager. (It also follows that if you *don't* understand networking, you may have a problem, as you don't know how your organization actually works!)

How they do it in China

Chinese businesspeople are some of the best networkers in the world, and what is more, they seem to have a natural flair for networking, though few can explain clearly how it is done. The Chinese term *guanxi* (gwan-shee) is usually translated in English as 'relationship' but more literally has connotations of 'open door'. If you have *guanxi* with someone, then their door is open to you; if you do not, then you may find the door is closed. Tim Ambler of London Business School, who has written extensively on *guanxi* and its applications in business in both China and the West, has commented that *guanxi* with customers, employees and suppliers is an essential pre-requisite to doing business in China.

The Chinese are explicit about *guanxi* for cultural reasons. Chinese culture was and remains strongly family oriented, and stresses relationships between family members as an important, even the most important, aspect of social life. The Confucian philosophical system, which still pervades much Chinese thinking, uses the family as a metaphor for many other social relationships, including business (and the Chinese are explicit too about seeing businesses as networks of – often hierarchical – relationships). In the West, especially in recent decades, the primacy of the individual has come to dominate much of our thinking; we see our rights as individuals as often being more important than our responsibility to others.

This is not the beginning of a lecture on ethics (though ethics do come into it), but rather a comment that too many of us think in terms of 'I', when we should be thinking of 'we'. Seeing a network of relationships as a community or a group with roughly common interests is the first step to successful networking. Thinking of yourself as one member of the group, as well as an individual, is another important point. Remembering that networks require you to give as well as take is yet another.

I come back to my original point, that good networking is an attitude of mind, a philosophy even, and it is founded on understanding of and respect for other people. It then requires an ability to identify common interests among that group. This is usually easy: on an MBA programme for example, most students will have a common aim – achieving success in the profession of management – even if their routes to that aim are quite different. Finally, it requires an understanding of what all members of that group or community have to contribute to one another, and this crucially involves knowing what you can give to other people as well as what they can do for you.

Relationships and networks are not simple tit-for-tat exchanges. Although the long-term aim is mutual benefit for all members, in the short term, apparently altruistic behaviour may be required. If another member of the network asks you for a favour, there may be no apparent *quid pro quo*. You may have to take it on trust that benefit will accrue. Most often, it does. One friend of mine, a consultant, took one of his contacts out to lunch once a year and paid the bill. This went on for some eight years without result; then, out of the blue the contact telephoned and offered my consultant friend several million pounds worth of work. In another case, a shipping friend tells of an acquaintance who, as a favour to one of his contacts, went off to attend what he thought would be a dull and uninteresting lunch. Several hours later, he emerged from the lunch as the exclusive broker for one of the world's largest shipping fleets. The Bible has a phrase for it: 'casting bread upon the waters'. Do things for other people and in most cases they will in turn do things for you.

Networks and ethics

Networks can of course be exploitative. This can happen in two ways, both of which need to be guarded against. First, networks can involve the exploitation of members by other members. Second, they can become secretive closed shops, and this can lead to corruption.

I mentioned above that respect for the dignity of others is an essential part of networking. One cannot view people as a commodity; people in your network do not have price tags stamped on their foreheads, or barcodes tattooed on their arms. There are limits to what people will willingly do, and coercion of someone in your network should be regarded as a strategy of last desperation; the relationship can only suffer. Also, people's privacy must be respected. Just because you have a professional relationship with someone does not give you rights to details of their private life. Whether a business relationship becomes a personal friendship is something that must happen naturally (though it is generally true that it is easier to network with people you like).

The issue of corruption is more difficult. Personal networks such as the 'old boy network' widely believed to run the City of London (finding evidence of this is another matter, by the way) are accused of prejudicing the system in favour of those who are members of the network against those who are not. Preferential treatment for jobs is a commonly cited case. This is obviously great if you are in the network, but rather less fun if you are not.

Hiring people on the basis of your knowledge of them, including your knowledge of how they work and that they will form a good partnership with you, is actually quite a good way of getting the right person into the right job. The problem occurs when an inferior candidate is preferred over superior ones solely on the grounds of their membership of a given network. This clearly is to be avoided as, obviously, do illegal activities such as insider trading and outright corruption. A large body of law and regulation exists to prevent these, but they can also be avoided through the application of basic standards of decency and a modicum of common sense. Networks do *not* automatically lead to corruption.

Adventure weekends

Many MBA programmes now feature an 'adventure weekend' (other names are often used as well) at some point in the programme. Indeed, more sadistic programme directors are now making participation in these mandatory. Adventure weekends, to those unfamiliar with the term, are excursions to camps or bases in the great outdoors, where students will undertake various exercises such as abseiling down rock faces, hikes across rugged moorland, orienteering exercises and that perennial favourite, making a raft to cross a river out of some old barrels and a few lengths of nylon rope. If all the rafts built by all the MBA students in the last decade were laid end to end, they would bridge the Atlantic.

Adventure weekends are meant to promote networking and team building. This is – to use a word with a long and honourable history in management jargon – bullshit. No one ever learned to network by building a raft; or bungee-jumping, or firewalking, or sitting in a sweat lodge, or any of the other myriad activities dreamed up at these centres. I doubt very much if they do much for team building either; the sheer pointlessness of most of the exercises inevitably saps the enthusiasm of some, if not all, of the team members.

There are some good reasons for going on adventure weekends. First, you may not be able to avoid it. Second, they are good outlets for the release of physical energy, and they do make a break from the grind of the programme, so go by all means for social reasons. Third, you may actually want to do some of these daft things. Finally, of course, there is peer pressure. If you do go, good luck. Break a leg, as they say in the theatre.

Networking and the MBA

Many MBA programmes have formal devices for promoting networking. Some offer networking skills courses as electives. Try these if you have a spare elective slot and are concerned about the level of your skills; the quality can vary, but you may learn some useful tips, at least. There is also the ubiquitous adventure weekend, one of the purposes of which is to promote 'bonding'. The best formal networking, though, occurs in those aspects of the MBA experience that this book has been discussing: courses, working in teams, project groups, classroom discussions and interactions with other students and faculty.

Making it happen

Networking will probably begin on or about the first day of the programme. The incoming student will meet and be introduced to colleagues in various courses and also to the faculty who teach on them. Some of the names won't stick in the memory, but never mind; the foundations have been laid.

Next steps come as the first few sessions of each course go on. Gradually you will get to know your colleagues, especially those with whom you are assigned to work or study in groups. Here are a few suggestions for enhancing the process:

- Concentrate on memorizing names or faces when you are introduced. Pick out some feature of the person that will remind you of who they are when next you meet. Be sure to acknowledge people you have met in class when you see them outside. Neither of you may remember who the other is, but a brief and tactful self-introduction can get over this.
- Be a good listener; get people to talk about themselves and their interests, even if only superficially. Build up a little bank of information about each person.
- Establish an address book early on, and keep people's names and contact details handy. Make little notes about them as aides-memoire, if it will help. 'John Smith, from California, engineer, went to UCLA' will be useful when looking up potential sources of information later. Remember, though, to respect the other person's privacy.
- Collect business cards, and always carry a few with you so you can reciprocate if someone gives you a card. If you have run out or left yours at home, give them a card when

next you meet, or put one in their mailbox with a note reminding them of who you are. This is especially important for part-time and Executive MBAs who will have their own professional cards as well as those supplied by the business school.

By the end of the first few weeks, the incoming student will have establish tentative links with a fair number of colleagues through the formal settings of the course. These can be enhanced through informal social contacts (see below). The next step will inevitably come when, at some point, the student needs help or assistance. Taking the resource-based view of the MBA we outlined in Chapter 1, the student reviews the possible resources in turn. He or she may need a professional opinion from a peer, or need background information about a particular subject and realize that a fellow student would almost certainly know. The choice is made to contact a colleague rather than one of the other resources.

Now the network becomes active. The first step is to initiate the contact. Here the term *depth*, referred to above, becomes important. How well do you know the person? Can you simply telephone them at home and ask, or would an e-mail be better? Should you ask the question outright over the phone or e-mail, or suggest a meeting to discuss it face-to-face? The answer depends in part on the complexity of the question asked or the favour needed, but also on the nature of the personal relationship. Close friends are less likely to be offended by a telephone call in the middle of supper than are formal professional acquaintances such as faculty supervisors.

Once the contact is initiated, state the request. The best policy then is usually to let the contact handle it in his or her own way. Remember, this person is doing you a favour, and you may not offering much by way of return. Respect his or her right to help you (or not) as he or she sees fit.

This exchange will be followed by other such. Meanwhile, other colleagues will also turn to you for help. Gradually, the interchange of information and ideas will begin to pick up speed. You will begin to know who you can rely on and feel closest to in professional and even personal terms. You will learn which of

IMPERCEPTIBLY, MANAGEMENT NETWORKING
LED TO RELATIONSHIP NETWORKING

your colleagues have most to offer you, and which ones you can be most helpful to. Imperceptibly, a network will emerge.

Is that all there is to it?

Yes and no. Essentially, networking is simple; it is, as noted earlier, a state of mind, a condition in which people with mutually coinciding interests feel that they can call on one another for favours, assistance, knowledge and support. Psychologically and in personal terms, it is complicated. Other people have the rights to make demands on you, and those demands may not always be convenient. When asked an inconvenient question, a choice must be made: do you refuse and prejudice the network, or do you agree and inconvenience yourself?

In fact, these are the sorts of choices we make in daily life on a regular basis, and only the most socially maladjusted of us would choose the same option every time. Networking is about people, and the relations between them. In professional as in personal life, not everything will be sweetness and light all the time. Respect for other people's dignity, ego and *amour-propre* must be a constant resonating theme in any networking activity.

Networking and social life

Important and vital though course work and projects are, MBA students should never forget to have a social life. All work and no play makes for a dull MBA.

Social life has a great deal of importance, and the opportunities it affords for networking must surely top the list. Getting to know your colleagues in a social situation is an excellent way to learn more about them, their habits, interests and general knowledge. Social networking is a very valuable complement to professional networking. A shared enjoyable social experience, such as a party or dinner, can be a good icebreaker in professional situations. As mentioned above, it is a lot easier to have a professional relationship with someone you like personally. (It isn't impossible to have a good professional relationship with someone you dislike, but it is harder and less fun; the mutual shared interests have to be pretty strong to make it work for long.)

Social life has other benefits too. It offers opportunities to rest and recharge the batteries, and so avoid the perils of over-concentration and tunnel vision. It helps develop a sense of perspective; seeing your colleagues as people instead of as cogs in the MBA programme's machine is better for your state of mind and for your relationships with others. Finally, social life broadens the mind. This is particularly true if you are doing an MBA in a different city or country from the one where you normally live and work. There is no better way to acquire knowledge about another culture than to live there for a while, as we will discuss in Chapter 11, and socializing with the natives is both a very efficient and quite fun way of gathering background knowledge.

How to have a social life

Well, someone was bound to ask. In fact, most MBA programmes are full of opportunities for social life. Bigger schools have ongoing clubs catering for many different special interests; consider joining one of these or, if there is no club that you like, starting your own. Most MBA programmes also have regular sporting events such as inter-campus football and rugby matches, golf tournaments and so on. Find regular partners for tennis or squash, or people to run, row, swim or work out with. Most programmes have regular programme-wide social events, like London Business School's Summer Ball or University of Capetown's Sunrise Club (participants go to an all-night party, then have to stay awake and alert through lectures the next day). Make a point of joining in some of these.

Use professional events as excuses for social ones. MBA programmes are expensive, but a few drinks or the odd lunch will not break the bank. At the end of a course, if you have got on particularly well, pool your money and go out for dinner; you might even want to consider inviting course faculty as well (some of them can be quite interesting and amusing when off duty). In-company project teams will usually benefit from the occasional lunch meeting too, especially if there is a way of charging this to expenses.

Having an active social life is part of the MBA experience. It helps the experience to be more rewarding and fun. It helps to transform professional relationships into personal friendships. Above all, it keeps your feet on the ground and reminds you that your colleagues, and you yourself, are still part of the human race. In the isolated, hothouse atmosphere of most MBA programmes, these are things worth remembering.

Part-time MBAs

For part-time and Executive MBAs there is usually less immediate pressure to develop a social life. Because personal lives are less dislocated, it is usually possible to carry on with previously existing social groups. Two observations are nonetheless in order.

First, if at all possible, make some attempt to develop social contacts with fellow students, even if on a very casual basis. This is a good idea because, as stated above, good personal relations usually help to oil the wheels of professional networks.

Second, the time pressures on part-time MBAs are usually much greater than those on full-time MBAs. The former have to hold down a job while at the same time working to a programme schedule only slightly less intense than that of the full-timers. These pressures make it all to easy too get sucked into a cycle of work–study–work–study (with occasional moments of sleep tucked in along the way). Take time off when possible; go out for a dinner or see a movie. The break should serve to make you more effective when you return to both work and study.

Spouses and partners

MBAs who are married or in long-term relationships, and especially those with children, need to recognize that the programme will make demands not only on them but on spouses, partners and families. This is a major issue, and it is something which should ideally be discussed well in advance of the programme. Again, the responsibility for dealing with this should not be all on one side.

Spouses and partners can choose to see the MBA as a sacrifice on their part; or they can see it as an opportunity for themselves.

Most MBA social events are open to spouses and partners, and thus offer them the opportunity to meet new people and develop new relationships/networks of their own. I know of husbands and wives of MBAs who have made valuable personal and professional contacts through meeting fellow students of their spouses. The same applies to going abroad, whether for the entire programme or on exchange. This can be an enriching experience for the whole family, not just for the student taking the MBA, provided everyone in the relationship is prepared to make the experience work for them.

Obviously, the dynamics of these relationships depend on the people involved. Making an MBA work in family situation, particularly if there are small children involved, can be difficult and sometimes hair-raising. But I do strongly urge spouses and partners to use the MBA experience for their benefit as well. Whether this means making new contacts or just gathering experiences from living and working in new places, there is valuable learning to be had by all.

After the programme

There is space for just a brief word about post-programme networking. The primary vehicle for this is the alumni association. Every business school worth the money has one of these, and alumni associations have the potential, at least, to be blue-chip networks, spanning the globe and including people in all sorts of companies and at every level up to and including chairman.

As this book is aimed at people embarking on an MBA, I shall content myself with a single observation about your school's alumni association: join it. A finer networking opportunity will never emerge. Over and over again I hear of how people who found that otherwise complete strangers, who were nonetheless members of the same alumni association, had come to their aid with vital contacts, knowledge, introductions and so on. Networking gets no better than this. So, attend alumni events and seminars; get to know people who came through the programme before and after yourself. If you don't find you are getting the value you should or if your local alumni group is badly organized, think about getting involved. The effort you put in will be repaid many times over.

A cautionary tale

A friend of a friend who graduated from Stanford grew tired of being pestered by his alumni association for donations (this is, I regret to say, one of the downsides of membership of an alumni association). Finally, wishing to cut all ties, he returned a letter from the association with the message that the person being addressed had deceased.

Years later, wishing to reactivate his links with the university for professional reasons and completely forgetting his earlier subterfuge, he wrote and applied to join his alumni association. His application was refused. Accordingly to information previously received, the association said, the applicant was already dead. Therefore the application was being treated as fraudulent.

Benefit maximization

As this chapter has argued, the ability (or skill, if you prefer) to network is a major asset to any modern manager. The MBA programme is full of opportunities, formal and informal, for networking. It follows that this is an ideal time not only to cultivate a network but also to develop the ability to manage it.

The two are co-terminous; the only real way to become good at networking is to do it. Practise networking on the MBA programme by meeting and talking to colleagues, formally and in social situations. This is probably the easiest networking you will ever do, as you have in effect a captive audience; your colleagues are there for the same purpose as yourself, you are in close proximity to them, and a community of interest will develop naturally. Later networking will require much more effort to make and develop contacts. Nonetheless, the skills developed on the programme will stand you in good stead later.

In terms of the MBA experience, networking is an essential part. Cultivating the networks themselves and the ability to create them will provide you with two powerful assets in your later career in management.

Conclusions

Networking is both nebulous and vitally important. Hard to define and teach, it is, I believe, quite easy to learn. Practice is essential, as is the ability to be outgoing and to develop relationships with people. Some people find this easy, others have to work harder; it is all down to personality. There are no hard and fast rules, though, and it is up to each person to work out how best to develop and manage networks.

In terms of the MBA, networking is one of the great benefits; some students I talk to say it is *the* most important benefit of the programme. Do not neglect it. The effort you put in now will be repaid many times over later in your career.

One of the best opportunities for networking that any student is likely to get is offered by the exchange programme. How this works and the benefits it provides are described in the next chapter.

Chapter 11

Exchange programmes

Travel, in the younger sort, is a part of education; in the elder, a part of experience. He that travelleth into a country before he hath some entrance into the language, goeth to school, and not to travel.
Sir Francis Bacon

This is a short chapter. In fact, it could be even shorter. As far as exchange programmes are concerned, my views are as follows. If your school offers the opportunity of an exchange, particularly with an overseas business school: *take it*.

Thank you. You may now turn to Chapter 12.

Choosing an exchange school

Exchange programmes are devices whereby students can spend a period of time, often one term, at another business school. The aim is to allow them to experience education and life in another culture. Most business schools have links with a number of other business schools around the world. Details of how to apply for the exchange programme are available from your own MBA programme office. In most cases you will be invited to apply for an exchange place, stating your preferred exchange school; as places may be limited, you may need to consider second and third preferences as well.

It follows that in choosing an exchange programme, it is important to pick one where the cultural experience will be quite different from where you are currently studying. If you are at a business school in New York, there would be little point in going on exchange to a school in Philadelphia; consider Patagonia instead.

When choosing from the menu of available schools, look for ones in regions where you have an interest, or where you think you will be able to acquire valuable cultural and language skills. The most popular exchanges are between Europe and America, or between schools in Northern and Southern Europe. Students at Asian business schools often choose to come to Europe or America, while a few adventurous Westerners go on exchange to Japan, Singapore or China.

Study target schools carefully before making your final choice. Look at the quality of the education on offer, and consider schools with courses which would add to your current stock of knowledge and complement courses you have already taken. Many schools will offer courses with a specialist local flavour, and these can be valuable. It is important too to maintain an educational standard which suits your own learning needs. Look at the schools' brochures and programme syllabus; if possible, talk to students who have been to the schools in question. Your own MBA programme office can usually give advice as well.

But the quality of the education received on an exchange programme is usually of secondary importance to the quality of the broader experience. Going on exchange to schools located in cultures with which you are not familiar will maximize the learning experience; but only if you are capable of fitting in. Be aware of your own abilities and limitations in areas such as language, for example. Try to find an exchange school where you think you will be able to fit in and meet people. A lot of this depends on your own personality and tastes, of course.

In practical terms, look for things like quality of accommodation (does the school provide this, or will you need to arrange your own?) and facilities. Look also for accessibility; a foreign business school stuck in the middle of nowhere will offer fewer chances for learning about local culture than one which is close to the centre of a major metropolis. At least part of your time on the exchange programme should be spent in exploring your environment, so make sure travelling around is feasible.

A few other considerations might also apply. Does the school have any noted academics whose opinions you might want to gather and listen to? Is it close to the headquarters of a major company in which you have a special interest? Are there

AT THE TIME IT SEEMED A WONDERFUL
OPPORTUNITY TO FINISH MY MBA
IN AN EXOTIC LOCATION

opportunities to do more project work of a kind which you want to be involved in? All these can be important, and taken together the arguments might indeed provide a compelling case for moving from New York to Philadelphia. But the cross-cultural experience is still the most valuable aspect of exchange programmes, and should be sought whenever possible.

Cross-cultural learning

Globalization is a fact of life for nearly every business, of whatever size and in whatever sector, in the world today. Firms source components and sell to customers around the world, and even smaller firms increasingly are tending to operate in a number of different countries and cultures simultaneously. The current trend towards cross-national alliances and mergers is making the ability to manage in different cultures even more valuable, although of course this trend might reverse itself at some point in the future.

The main point is that to be successful in modern management, managers must be able to work in cultures other than their own. Also, they must be able to do what is known as 'managing across boundaries', which means managing in organizations which span different cultures. When studying globalization, you will probably hear a lot about global convergence, by which is meant that globalization is gradually ironing out the differences between cultures and steering us towards one homogenous culture. This trend may really be happening, but its effects are patchy and do not apply equally to everyone everywhere; there is still a long way to go. In the meantime, the ability to manage between and across cultures will remain a necessity.

As with networking, I am not sure that cross-cultural management is really a skill. Again, it is more of a state of mind. Its foundations are understanding of and respect for other people's cultures, an appreciation of the similarities *and* the differences between cultures, and an ability to see how both the similarities and the differences can be used positively when networking and managing.

Before going on an exchange programme, students should make themselves familiar with the essentials of the culture in which the host school is located. Don't overdo this; half a dozen sources will probably do the trick. Read the relevant Economist Intelligence Unit country report, a couple of good travel books and one of the more intelligent travel guides, such as *Lonely Planet*. If possible, read a couple of novels or see some films made in the country in question. All these things will give you a flavour, and prepare you for some of what to expect when you arrive.

Desk research is useful, but it can only take you so far. Ultimately, the best way to learn about cross-cultural management is to live in and experience other cultures. That is why the exchange programme is so very valuable. It represents a crash course in another culture, and provides the basic foundational knowledge about that culture. Also, to survive an exchange programme, you need to develop and expand those very attributes which we described above: respect, tolerance, an appreciation and admiration of difference and diversity. You need to learn not just what other people do, but also how they think, what mental models of the world and other people they carry around with them, and how this affects their view of the world (and you).

The joy of getting it right

A lot of otherwise competent managers have problems managing cross-culturally. Sometimes personal psychological and social factors are to blame for this, but the most common problems are lack of confidence and lack of experience. The two are of course interrelated; confidence in dealing with other cultures usually grows out of experience.

Being confident and able to work with managers, customers, employees, suppliers and so on from cultures other than your own is intensely rewarding on many levels. In professional terms, successful cross-cultural managers usually have doors opened to them that may remain shut to more parochial colleagues. There is also the simple thrill of success; cross-cultural management is more challenging, and so getting it right is more pleasing. On a personal level, managing across international boundaries offers opportunities to see and learn from the rich diversity of the world's peoples. There are downsides; air travel will never be anything more than uncomfortable at best, and there can be personal and family problems involved in relocation and working as an expatriate. Generally, though, the rewards should outweigh the difficulties.

Doing courses

While on the exchange programme, you will usually be expected to take a full load of courses and participate fully in the life of the host business school. Some schools are tougher on this than others; some accept that exchange students will spend a fair amount of time exploring and learning on their own, while others insist that the educational aspects of the experience should take priority.

As stated above, the courses offered by host schools are probably of less importance overall than the chance to live and learn in a foreign culture. But this does *not* mean they are irrelevant. The advice here is to take as many courses as you can, participate fully in discussions, study groups and other work, and work as hard as you would at your home school. Difficulties may be encountered; there may be language barriers, or teaching methods may be rather different from what you are used to. Overcome these as best you can, and learn what is available from the experience. Many business schools offer elective courses in particular which are tailored to local markets and operating environments, and these are bound to be good sources of knowledge.

There is also the contribution which you yourself can make in class and in work groups. Coming from overseas, you will bring different kinds of knowledge, different perspectives and different ideas. Bringing these into discussions and analysis will be a valuable learning experience for your colleagues at the host school, who will also respect your for your commitment and willingness to 'pitch in' and work with them. This in turn can have a positive effect on your ability to network.

Opportunities for networking

The final great benefit of exchange programmes is the opportunity they offer for further extending your network. Exchange programmes last only a few months or weeks, so time will be short. But by energetically cultivating the networking abilities you have already been developing in your home school (see Chapter 10), you can develop potentially very valuable contacts in your new milieu. This is particularly important if you are planning to live and work in this culture at some point in the future; keeping in touch with your new contacts in the intervening period means you will have a support network in place when you arrive back on the scene.

Networking across cultures can be hard work. Language, particularly idiomatic language, often gets in the way and can cause misunderstandings. Forms of etiquette and social behaviour can also cause confusion, and no matter how much you study beforehand, you are bound to drop at least one 'clanger' during the course of the exchange. Tact, respect and dignity are essential elements of a successful exchange programme, and are particularly necessary when networking overseas.

Other exchange students

You are unlikely to be the only exchange student on the programme, and there may well be other students from your country, even your own school. This can be very useful, as the exchange students can often support one another and pool knowledge in an effort to overcome any problems they may have in adjusting to their new environment. However, it is probably not a good idea to form a real 'exchange students' club'. Socialize with your own group by all means, but mix in with the home school's students as well; you will learn much more in the end from them.

Problems and drawbacks

We have suggested some of these above. Working and living in a strange culture is seldom easy, at least to start with. Even in supposedly related cultures such as those of the USA and the UK there are plenty of pitfalls for the unwary, even in the use of language and everyday speech (was it George Bernard Shaw who described Britain and America as 'two nations divided by a common language'?). Getting to know the basics, like how to get around by public transport and where to go for food and entertainment, all takes time and can be discouraging if there are repeated problems.

On a more general level, there will always be a cultural gap to be overcome. Some cultures place a premium on politeness and personal reserve, and it can be hard to get to know people quickly. Patience, as well as tact, will be required.

Knowledge management

Also while on exchange, students should continue to use and develop their knowledge management skills. In terms of knowledge acquisition, the new environment will offer many rich opportunities. Knowledge can be acquired not only from the standard resources such as libraries and information centres, faculty and other students, but also from simple observation of one's environment. Knowledge organization is then essential to make sure that all this new knowledge is retained and can be recalled when wanted, particularly on return to the home school. Finally, knowledge use comes into play both when you apply previous knowledge to the analysis of new experiences, and on return to the home school when the knowledge gained on exchange is used when working on new problems.

The exchange programme should certainly broaden and deepen the knowledge you acquire from the MBA programme, but it should improve knowledge management skills and techniques as well. Put some effort into this; organize your notes, photos and files on your return home, and actively look for opportunities to use your new knowledge. As noted earlier in the book, knowledge, like a dog, needs regular exercise. Don't lose the opportunities provided by the exchange programme by letting your new knowledge go to waste.

Benefit maximization

The exchange programme can be an immensely positive and enriching experience. Going on an exchange is one of the ways in which the benefits provided by the programme can be maximized. The added bonuses of new knowledge, more and different contacts and the beginnings of a facility to manage cross-culturally will stand the student in good stead, professionally and personally.

At the same time, the experience of the exchange programme itself can be maximized by use of the skills and abilities which you have begun to develop in the course of your MBA programme. In earlier chapters we have discussed such things as teamworking, written and oral communication, research and analysis. Continuing to use these, both formally by getting involved in course work and informally by exploring your new environment and learning about the host culture, will bring more value to the exchange programme, and thus to the MBA programme as a whole.

Conclusions

This chapter has been a very brief look at exchange programmes and the value they provide. Exchange programmes have a number of features. They broaden the mind and increase knowledge. They offer many chances of networking and developing new contacts in different fields. They develop an understanding of and respect for other cultures which is one of the bases for success in cross-cultural management.

All these are assets which should greatly enhance the career prospects of any manager. In the next chapter, we turn to this critical issue, and discuss some of the considerations involved in seeking and finding a job after the programme is over.

Chapter 12

Getting a job
Recruitment during and after the programme

I like work; it fascinates me. I could sit and look at it for hours.
Jerome K. Jerome

One of the ultimate aims which nearly all MBA students have in mind when they embark on the programme is career enhancement. This is of course a general term, which can mean many things. Most full-time MBA students are looking for a career change and a chance to put themselves in the running for more senior positions; they are usually looking to be recruited by a new firm. Part-time and executive MBA students, on the other hand, may be looking for advancement within their own firm, or they may be motivated by the idea of changing employers and jobs at some point in the future.

Either way, the end of the programme means that students now have to market themselves and the knowledge they have acquired to prospective or current employers. MBA programme managers are aware of this, and provide a range of tools and resources for the use of graduating students. All, or nearly all, programme offices maintain a career resource centre or career advice centre which provides a range of facilities, from how to write a CV to tips and prospects for students seeking employment. These centres are among the most valuable resources an MBA programme has to offer, most are of very high quality with good links to recruiting companies, and they are free. Students should should use them as fully as possible.

Because these resources exist, this chapter does not go into detail on how to get a job. Instead, the focus is on one of the recurring themes of the book: maximizing value and ensuring that the graduate gets the *best* job, the one best suited to his or her own aims and goals. The aim on graduating should not be to get *a* job, but to get the *right* job.

The chapter begins with a discussion of what recruiting companies are looking for. It discusses the need to keep focused on personal and career goals, and presentation and the need for professionalism. A few notes then follow on what to look for in a recruiting company and on the best attitude to use when dealing with recruiters.

What are recruiters looking for?

The MBA programme provides a wide range of skills and knowledge to its graduates, and recruiters are properly appreciative of these. But ultimately, recruiters are looking at two things: the *person* and the *potential*.

Companies are a little like vampires. They constantly need fresh blood. More importantly, they need people who they think may be capable of leading them into the future. They want fresh intellects, new ideas, new perspectives. Any MBA graduate who comes into a company will be entered into its human resources database as a possible future leader.

Fifty years ago, recruitment was simple. A graduate was matched with a recruiting company and, if the terms were acceptable, joined up. Most then spent their remaining careers with the same firm, retiring at 60 having reached the board or come very near it, with the standard pension and gold watch or carriage clock.

Careers do not work that way these days. There is little or no job security, and the senior manager is as likely to be downsized as the shopfloor worker. This is the age of what Charles Handy calls the 'portfolio career', when managers jump from job to job seeking to move up the ladder with each move, and when companies pick and choose in the job market in an effort to secure the best available talent for the job in hand.

In other words, graduates seeking jobs are no longer looking for jobs for life; they are looking for the next step in their career progression. The step after that may be with the same firm, or it may be somewhere else. Likewise, companies are not looking at MBAs as automatic candidates for the main board of directors. They are looking for people who have the *potential* to succeed. There will be many more tests in the future, and those who did not fit exactly with the company's needs will find at some point in the future that there is no call for their services.

That may sound harsh, and may indeed be a bit disappointing for those assuming that the MBA is their ticket to the boardroom. But it is as well to be realistic. In today's environment, the MBA is a step up – and a very big one – in a manager's career, but there are many other steps to be taken. The MBA is not a complete summary of the knowledge required for top management; rather, it is the first step on the road to lifelong learning (see Chapter 13).

So, recruiting companies are looking for potential. You, as an MBA graduate, will definitely have potential. How do you go about communicating this and attracting the attention, not just of any company, but the one you want to work for?

Self-employment

Not every MBA graduate goes to work for a big firm; some go straight into business for themselves. For these people, this chapter may seem less relevant, but it is probably worth a read nonetheless. The key points to getting a job are the right attitude, focus on goals, and an attention to professionalism. The self-employed graduate does not need to impress these qualities on potential recruiters. He or she will, however, need to deal with investors, venture capitalists, bankers and partners in order to get the chosen business off the ground. In order to be persuaded to part with the necessary money and other resources, these same qualities will be required.

Whether getting a job or raising capital for one's own venture, the keys are *professionalism* and *presentation*. This chapter discusses both.

I WOULD OF COURSE KEEP YOU ON AS CHIEF EXECUTIVE

Focusing on goals

As with every aspect of the MBA programme, the first principle when searching for a job or seeking promotion within an existing career structure is to focus on personal and professional aims. Where does the graduate want to be in five, ten, fifteen, twenty years? What sort of job does he or she want to be doing? What is the ultimate career aim?

These are questions that should be asked even before the programme begins – ideally even before the decision to seek an MBA is finally taken. However, the answers to these questions should not be regarded as fixed or set. One of the purposes of the MBA should be to broaden horizons, and it is almost inevitable that personal and career goals will change and evolve under the impact of the new learning that the programme brings. Not directly discussed in this book but probably important is a very special kind of knowledge which comes out of the MBA: self-knowledge.

Near the end of the programme, these goals should reviewed. For the full-time MBA or other student seeking a new job, this review process should aim to both rehearse the goals themselves and concentrate the mind on the job search ahead. For part-timers and others planning to stay within an existing career structure, this review is less necessary but nonetheless valuable. Examining one's goals again in the light of new knowledge may well serve to confirm previous views; or it may suggest new directions.

What to look for in a recruiting company

Recruitment is not a one-way street, and when searching for a job students should try to match up with companies whose profiles match their own interests as closely as possible.

There are some obvious things to watch out for. What is the company's reputation like? Do they treat their staff and managers well? Are the pay and bonus structures in line with the rest of the industry? What are the promotion prospects? Does the company support further education and training for managers? (A critical one this; see Chapter 13.) Is the company likely to remain solvent in the near future?

The answers to some of these questions (though not usually the last) can be gained through direct inquiry of recruiters and other company representatives. For others, you might have to ask around. Use your network to find contacts who work or have worked for the firm. Try to find out things like the rate of managerial turnover and the length of time managers can expect to stay in one job before receiving promotion. In other words, it is not just the job on offer that matters; it is future prospects.

Look too at what the company does, and especially its track record in terms of performance and innovation. When in five or six years' time you consider making a move to another firm, how will the first company's name look on your CV? Will further recruiters consider you as a talented manager on the make, or as a refugee from a bad situation? This attitude will affect your value in the job market, including the kinds of jobs and the salaries you will be offered.

Finally, and this may be personal prejudice of my own, but don't focus too strongly on companies in 'trendy' industries. At time of writing, MBAs are queuing up to join e-commerce companies, largely on account of the mega-bucks allegedly to be made in this world. If, as is quite possible, 90 per cent of these firms go belly-up in the next few years, there are going to be a lot of unemployed MBAs washing around the system, while meanwhile new crops of graduates with even more up-do-date skills will be creaming off the best jobs. If e-commerce really interests you, then go ahead and good luck. But don't dive into untried or untested businesses without considering the likelihood and consequences of failure.

You are a professional, going into a professional's world. You have an impressive battery of skills and knowledge at your command. As a graduate from an MBA programme, you are capable of meeting many managerial challenges. Do not sell yourself short, in terms of the job you take or the firm you go to work for. Demand the best, and expect to get it. If you settle for a dead-end job, then much of the MBA experience may be wasted.

Presentation and professionalism

As well as the advice offered by MBA schools' career resource centres, there are plenty of books and articles on how to go about seeking a job, and plenty of consultant agencies who will offer (for a fee) to help you. Use the business schools' own centres first, largely because they are free. Don't bother going outside unless you really are havng trouble finding what you want.

The main principle behind any sort of job seeking or career planning is to adopt a professional approach. This is particularly the case when seeking to present oneself to a company, either in writing through an application letter or curriculum vitae (CV), or in person at an interview.

CVs

There are various ways of structuring a CV, but the classic method – personal details, followed by details of education, followed by relevant work experience – is still the best. It has the advantage of familiarity – recruiters know how to read this format and extract the information they need – and brevity. A good CV is nearly always as short as possible; unless you have a long list of professional accomplishments or publications, 3-4 pages should be the absolute maximum. A headhunter of my acquaintance used to receive CVs from American students of thirty pages or more in length, including one which began memorably, 'I was born on a small farm in...' Needless to say, this and others like it went straight into the rubbish bin.

CVs should be brief and terse, conveying the maximum information in the minimum space. They should also look professional, being properly laid out on the page and easy to read, but with a minimum of flourish. Coloured inks and paper should be avoided; give recruiters your life details in, literally, black and white. When constructing the CV itself, give the details in the format suggested by the guidebooks; nearly all say the same thing, and there is no point in repeating it here.

As with all forms of written communication, remember to put yourself in the mind of the reader. Once you have drafted the CV, read through it again, pretending you are a complete stranger reading this document for the first time. What does this say about the person being described? Is it fair and accurate? Does it fully describe that person's potential? In general, where CVs tend to go wrong is in underselling rather than overselling the candidate. Be brief but fair and confident about your own abilities. Most of all, make sure that the CV shows your capabilities and your *potential* as a manager.

Interviews and testing

Many of the same principles apply to job interviews and other selection procedures and tests. If you go for many of these, you will find they are something of a mixed bag. Some companies approach interviewing and other selection procedures with a very professional attitude and focus on the candidate. Others have some distinctly odd notions. I once went for an interview with a *very* large management consultancy firm, to discover that the entire interview consisted of filling out a multiple choice aptitude test. Turning the document over, I discovered that it had a copyright date of some 35 years previously. It all asked questions about subjects such as American vice-presidents and NASA moon missions, which since I was then in London I thought was distinctly odd. And it gets even odder (see box below).

More commonly, one finds one is being interviewed by someone who does not really appear to know what interviewing is about. Be patient, though, and play along. There is always the chance that this is a bluff. More seriously, losing patience with the person from HR who has come along to see you could put in jeopardy an otherwise good job with an otherwise good company. Never judge a recruiter on the basis of first impressions.

Be aware too that the process going on in an interview is not just a case of you selling yourself to the recruiter. The chances are that the company is also trying to sell itself to you. By the time you get to the interview, you will have already been through several stages of the selection process, and will have been identified as having at least some potential; therefore, the company already has an interest in you. This is flattering, or can be, but one must remain realistic. Joining a company just because they are nice to you is not necessarily the best thing; it can easily lead to the wrong job with the wrong firm at the wrong time. Once again, stay focused on your goals.

Astrologers and witch-doctors

You may, as I say, encounter some very odd things indeed when searching for a job. According to a recent BBC news report, 10 per cent of all firms in the city of London employ a graphologist to analyse samples of handwriting from potential applicants. A graphologist is a handwriting analyst who claims to be able to tell details of a person's character from his or her handwriting; for example, writing which slopes strongly to the right is considered to indicate a strong forceful character. (Presumably, left-handed people need not apply.) The report did not make clear how many firms employ the services of an astrologer, *feng shui* master, druid or witch-doctor in their selection processes, but presumably the number is substantial.

There is no point in kicking against this, and you may as well go along with it, assuming you still want to work for the firm in the first place. Play the game and try to get in front of an interview panel, when you will have a chance to let your skills and personality speak for themselves.

Above all, be professional. Treat the interview seriously; be well groomed and punctual and let the interviewers manage the process. Candidates who talk too much or who show up the panel are as likely to be thrown out as those who fail to make any impression at all. Be judicious in your views, honest in the information you provide and polite in your mode of expression. If these rules are followed, the interview cannot go too badly wrong.

Recruiters are looking for a commodity. They want to buy management potential, for use in both the short-term and the long-term. Any presentation, be it a CV, interview or other test, must focus on selling that potential. Stress your own unique qualities and abilities. Make it clear that you cannot only do what the company asks of you, but much more; you can add value for them, and cannot only justify the money they spend recruiting and paying you, but make that back for the firm many times over. Confidence in your ability to do these things is the starting point for successful marketing of yourself as an MBA graduate to top firms.

Giving the right impression

Much of the process of seeking a job at the end of the MBA programme is about projecting the right attitude. A projection of confidence, intelligence and ability is required. However, these must also be expressed in moderation: confidence must stop short of arrogance, intelligence must not be seen as showing off.

The actual nature of this projection must of course depend on the character and personality of the individual graduate, but there are four key rules that should be followed at all times. The purpose of these to avoid underselling, which as mentioned above is far more common than overselling. These rules are the four 'don'ts' which follow below.

1   Don't appear as a supplicant. Never convey to a recruiter that you really *need* a job (even if you do). Make it clear that you are interested in the job on its merits because it fits your profile, and that you see interviews and selection panels as a meeting of equals.
2   Don't settle for second best unless you must. Getting trapped in the wrong job at the wrong time can set your career back years. Hold out for what you want. If you are good, you will get it; given time, your potential will be recognized.
3   Don't worry if your colleagues land jobs before you do. It doesn't matter. They might have got lucky; or, *they* might have settled for second best. Never mind peer pressure, there are no prizes for getting a job first. Wait until the right offer comes along.
4   Don't panic. Recruiters, even the dimmest of them, can smell fear. Be confident; if you are asked a question and you don't know the answer, say so. Bluffing is common in this game, and most HR people are good at spotting it.

Conclusions

For most MBAs, seeking a new job or promotion within an existing career structure is the primary purpose of joining the programme in the first place. Throughout this book it has been argued that MBAs should focus on personal as well as professional goals and should seek self-development as well as career enhancement. To a great degree, though, the two are co-terminous. Graduates who have achieved a high degree of self-development will be broad-minded, experienced, innovative thinkers with a wide range of skills. These are exactly the qualities that many recruiting companies are looking for in a manager.

In Chapter 1, we commented that recruiters are not so much looking for the MBA itself but for the kind of person who will take on and make a success of the MBA. In other words, they are less interested in past success than in the potential for future success. As a graduate, you must sell yourself not only on the basis of past achievements; you must also persuade recruiters that you are capable of much more.

Doing this requires you to demonstrate the many skills acquired through the MBA. Some of these can be described formally in a CV. Others will have opportunities to be shown during the selection process. Be alert to opportunities to demonstrate your own potential.

Above all, though, make sure that at the end of the programme you get the kind of job you want, which fits in with your career goals and which will help propel you towards the goals. Taking the wrong job at the wrong time can derail an otherwise promising career. Ultimately, a certain amount of selfishness is required. What career or job will see *you* make the best use of the MBA experience and your own talents?

One of the most important aspects to consider is the potential for lifelong learning, which is the subject of the next chapter. As we shall see, the MBA is just one step forward on the road to career success. Many others await.

Chapter 13

The MBA and lifelong learning

A journey of a thousand leagues starts from where your feet stand.
Daodejing

This chapter is about lifelong learning. Regarded as a faddish concept in the 1990s, lifelong learning is nonetheless a valuable theme to be aware of, and in the first decade of the twenty-first century most companies and most managers are taking it seriously. Throughout this book, we have stressed the importance of knowledge and learning in terms of competitive advantage, to companies and especially to managers. Those who can learn and manage knowledge will be more likely to succeed.

The MBA is thus not the end (or even the beginning of the end) of management education, but is rather a foundation for future learning and development. That should be thought of as an overarching theme to all activities on the programme. So, the most important skill which can be acquired or improved is *learning how to learn*.

Human capital – which is what we all are – is endlessly flexible and constantly changes. Knowledge and skills evolve and are dynamic. Learning is an ongoing process. This too has always been the case, but we are starting to understand the processes much better. The one certainty in our brave new world is that there are few certainties, at least so far as knowledge is concerned. The knowledge we regard as cutting edge now may well be obsolete in a few years. Acquiring and using new knowledge is not just about keeping up, it is also about staying ahead of the game.

What is lifelong learning?

Like many of the concepts described in this book, lifelong learning is a philosophy, a state of mind. It starts from the view that knowledge has a limited lifespan and must constant be refreshed, updated and replaced by new knowledge. To that end, managers must never stop learning. If they do, then like the 'dodo' described in Chapter 5, they will be obsolete, unable to understand or analyse their environment and unable to see a way forward, fit for nothing more than a second career in politics. (H. Ross Perot is a 'dodo' in this respect; analyse his career, and you will see what I mean.)

Lifelong learning has two aspects, formal training and informal learning. Formal training comes in many guises, and most large companies now have sizeable training departments devoted to planning, assessing and meeting individual training needs. Formal programmes range from one-off in-house seminars to full-scale formal programmes like the Sloan Fellowship programme offered at MIT, Stanford and London Business School, various MSc programmes in special disciplines, advanced executive programmes and even PhD programmes.

Most formal learning programmes have been carefully designed to fit in at various stages of a manager's career as he or she progresses upwards either through a single firm or, more commonly, along a zigzag path through many different firms. Going on these programmes is often a matter of three-cornered negotiation between the manager, his or her superiors and the firm's training department. Opportunities for formal training should be taken up where possible, so long as the training programme in question appears relevant to all parties.

Informal learning is learning which happens in everyday situations, at work, in social situations or at home. Informal learning is an ongoing process, which happens to most of us without being aware of it. There are ways of being proactive about informal learning. Subscribing to journals (and remembering to read them), setting up small informal research projects out of private interest and participating in in-company research and project teams are examples. Informal learning is a good way of advancing knowledge in small increments, gradually building up knowledge on particular subjects and, of course, exercising knowledge management skills.

Why is it important?

Once upon a time, a firm took full responsibility for its managers' training needs. The modern model of the portfolio career, however, means managers design their own career paths and therefore must take responsibility for their own training needs. Most firms recognize this, and many rely on managers to be proactive about their learning needs.

Managers have to think about learning, not just do it. An understanding of likely future needs must be built into any career plan; indeed, a separate learning plan might not be a bad idea. Of course it is impossible to tell exactly what one will need to know in five years' time, given the rapid advances in knowledge and changes in the business environment, but working out a broad-brush strategy should still be attempted.

The need for learning is sometimes presented solely as a need for managers to 'keep up' with changes in the business environment. This is necessary, of course, but adopting this as the end goal means that managers are at best kept abreast of whatever changes are taking place. A better strategy is to aim to get out from the middle of the herd. Learn faster than your colleagues and competitors, and you have an advantage over them. That, at least, is the management wisdom of today.

Examples of failures to adapt are abundant in business past and present. The canal companies failed to anticipate the development of the railway; the railway operators in turn failed to appreciate the impact of the motor car and the airplane. The history of IT development over the past several decades is littered with examples of firms who saw 'their' technology as being the summit of achievement, and failed to realize that the next technology was waiting around the corner to destroy them. Even the mighty Microsoft has its weaknesses in this regard; it adapted to Internet technology, but only just in time, and has it managed to respond to the advent of wireless application protocols (WAPs)? Time will tell. On the other hand, there are examples of companies that *have* responded to new generations of knowledge and turned them to account. Sun Microsystems is a good example. So, in its ponderous way, is IBM, still the only private sector company to have ever won a Nobel Prize for its research.

Innovation and creativity are the watchwords of today. To innovate, you must always be ahead of the game. But you cannot innovate without knowledge. Let us say it again: you must learn faster than your competitors. Continuous, lifelong learning is about to become, if it is not already, the most important management task.

What contribution does the MBA make to lifelong learning?

The MBA is of course only the first stage in a manager's lifelong learning. But it is of crucial importance because it lays the foundations of the lifelong learning programme. The fundamental skills and abilities developed on the MBA are the very skills and abilities needed to manage lifelong learning: research skills, communication skills, networking and teamworking abilities.

It is for this reason that this book has laid such stress on knowledge management as one of the most important, perhaps the most important, aspect of the MBA experience. Two points about knowledge management need to repeated and taken away.

First, lifelong learning and knowledge management are co-dependent terms. Knowledge management refers to the fact that managers' primary task is increasingly becoming the management and use of knowledge. But new knowledge is constantly required in order to keep ahead of the game. A programme of lifelong learning is thus essential to supply the required new knowledge.

Learning for managers is not something that comes and goes; it is a continuous, enduring process. This is why the MBA experience is so valuable. MBA programmes are intense, concentrated and continuous processes of knowledge management. But it should not be assumed that this process can stop once the student graduates from the programme and takes up or returns to a job. Rather, the process of knowledge management, especially knowledge acquisition, must continue.

It should be possible for students to transfer their knowledge management skills and techniques straight from the MBA into the job. Similarly, subsidiary skills and abilities – like research skills and oral and written communication skills – should transfer

LIFELONG LEARNING IS
ONE THING · · · · · ·

straight across. As this book has pointed out, all these skills require knowledge management. The ability to see knowledge management as part of the daily routine of management more generally, then, is one of the most important benefits of the MBA.

And it is not just skills that matter, but also the attitude of mind. The ability to see the bigger picture, to think globally, to manage across boundaries and across cultures; the ability to respect and understand other people; the ability to tolerate diversity and even make it work for you: these are all things which the MBA will help to develop. All these assets in turn will impact on future learning.

In the sixteenth century, the financier Jakob Fugger, the Bill Gates of his day, wrote that he did not go to bed each night until he had performed at least one business transaction that had turned a profit. Today's manager could adopt a similar maxim; no business day should be complete unless there had been some learning and knowledge management skills had been used in some way. (If this happens, then I submit that profit will follow of its own accord.) The MBA programme is a perfect training for this attitude of mind. The MBA is all about learning. Management should be also.

Conclusions

So the MBA, then, is not the end. It is not even, as Winston Churchill said, the beginning of the end. Learning is a lifelong process; knowledge management skills will always be needed, and will always be in a state of development. Rather, the MBA is a launchpad. It is a place where the lifelong learning process can be established, defined, understood and put into practice.

We are now looking into the future, when the MBA student has graduated, found the job which suits him or her, and embarked on a career in which managerial ability is based on knowledge management skills acquired on the MBA programme. This is, of course, the perfect outcome. So what can the reader of this book, perhaps thinking of embarking on an MBA, or about to start one, or already into the process, do to achieve this state of grace? The next chapter sums up.

Chapter 14

Conclusion
Broad vision, sharp focus

Let us bring this book to an end as succinctly as we can. Its purpose, as spelled out in the introduction, was to show ways in which MBA students could maximize the value they derive from the MBA programme, thus enhancing their personal attributes and professional skills. This in turn should lead to a greater chance for personal and career success.

Chapter 1 established two core concepts, *benefit maximization* and *knowledge management*. It discussed these in fairly abstract terms, showing why each was important and a little of how each works. Knowledge management in particular is a new concept for many managers, and MBAs who master it will have a great competitive edge. In fact, though, as the chapter and the rest of the book has been at pains to point out, the entire MBA programme is one continuous exercise in knowledge management. So, the student does not have to go out and 'start managing knowledge'; he or she is already doing it. Understand the process, and make it work for you.

Chapter 2 looked the importance of the setting-up stage and suggested ways in which students could organize themselves for learning. We suggested that one of the most important aspects of this phase was the setting aside of preconceptions and opening up one's mind and senses to learning from many sources.

Chapters 3–7 looked at formal coursework. Chapter 3 showed how courses are the formal structure on which the MBA is built, and discussed their different types and value. It was suggested that courses should be seen as the first and in some ways the most important channel through which knowledge is acquired. As such, they are of central importance to knowledge management on the programme. Chapter 4 looked at case studies, one of the major tools used on many courses, and Chapter 5 discussed some of the issues surrounding working in teams with other students.

Chapters 6 and 7 discussed written and oral communication and presentation, respectively. Chapter 6 took a pragmatic approach to writing, demystifying it and setting aside many of the rules. We noted that the primary criteria of effective writing is fitness for purpose – is the desired message conveyed to the desired audience – introduced the model AAMR (aim, audience, message, response) as a guide to understanding this process. Some practical aspects of writing were also touched on. Chapter 7 used the same model and discussed both formal classroom presentations and informal discussions. It was noted that interaction between students in the classroom is a way to not only exchange information but also to generate new learning.

Chapter 8 looked at research and some of the tools used in knowledge acquisition. Research and communication are simply two sides of the same coin; one without the other has little or no value. The chapter looked some of the sources and techniques for doing research, including how to analyse and examine the validity of data and how to present. Chapter 9 took research into the 'real world' by looking at in-company projects and also looking at some of the issues surrounding field research.

The next two chapters discussed some of the less obvious but highly valuable aspects of the MBA experience. Chapter 10 looked at the highly nebulous subject of networking, commonly cited by students as one of the most valuable – even *the* most valuable – benefit of the MBA programme. Chapter 11 discussed overseas exchange programmes and concluded that although these can be difficult, they are also sources of very great benefit in terms of experience, opportunities for networking, and the chance to learn some of the basics of cross-cultural management. Both networking and the exchange programme are excellent ways to add more value to the MBA experience.

The last two chapters showed some of the ways in which value emerges. In Chapter 12 we looked at the job search which often accompanies the end of the MBA programme, not in terms of the mechanics of the process but to show how the learning and value from the MBA programme could make this process yield more benefit for the student. Professonalism, presentation skills, the ability to research and learn about a potential recruiter, and above the ability to focus on and achieve a goal were seen as crucial to this process. Chapter 13 then briefly introduced the concept of lifelong learning. The MBA is clearly the first step on the road to lifelong learning, and it is important to see the skills and knowledge acquired on the programme not as ends in themselves but as essential pre-requisites for later learning and development. Continuous learning is a vital source of competitive advantage, for both the manager and his or her firm.

* * * * *

Is there one big idea which we can use to sum up this book? If there is any one concept which is of all-embracing importance, even more than knowledge management, even more than benefit maximization, I think it is the need for *purpose*. No student goes on an MBA programme without a purpose. The cost in terms of time and money is too great to make this a venture to be entered into lightly. Most people have some goal in mind.

But what is that goal? How sharply is it defined? Is the goal so clear that everything the student does on the programme can be seen as working towards that goal? If not, then it might be worth looking at the goal again. It is easy to set a goal; it is a lot harder to stay focused on it.

At the same time, is the goal flexible? One of the things the MBA programme does is open up new vistas, new horizons, new ideas. It is not uncommon for students to go into an MBA programme bent on a career in, say, management consultancy, only to discover that actually high-tech ventures or marketing in the Far East are far more exciting and equally lucrative. This involves changing horses in mid-stream; but a flexible mind and an ability to manage knowledge and focus on benefits and value can do it.

Parenthetically, this is one of the things that worries me about the current trend among US students to abandon their MBAs halfway through after receiving lucrative job offers from high-tech start-ups. Five years from now, where will they be? One in a hundred will be multi-millionaires. The other ninety-nine will be trying to get their careers back on track, and will be blown out of the water by the next generation of MBA graduates coming out with even better skills and more up-to-date knowledge...

I promised to be succinct. Here it is, then: the guiding principle which should serve not only the MBA programme but also all of a manager's subsequent career: *broad vision, sharp focus*.

Breadth of vision is essential. The MBA is mind-opening, and students should use it as a chance to expand the limits of their vision and their views of the world. This happens in all sorts of ways: examples include respect and tolerance of other cultures, an ability to see and understand the views of other people, an attitude to creativity which sees it as a way to solve problems, an ability to do research which breaks new ground, and an ability to communicate big ideas and manage networks of like-minded people. A successful MBA thinks big: thinks global, even. And every incident that comes through his or her career is a potential opportunity.

And thence comes the sharpness of focus. In the vast world of floating opportunities, it is essential to seize on what matters. Filter out the non-essentials; target what is important, and then work out a plan and a schedule to go after it. This is true whether pursuing one's employer's goals or one's own career advancement (and ideally, the two should be harmonious).

The MBA is (we say it one last time) a once-in-a-lifetime experience. This is your best chance to set your career on track and make things happen according to your own vision of the future. The programme offers you the chance to develop skills and abilities which will be essential to achieving that vision. But it is not a passport. You will need to work hard, to maximize the value you gain, and to present that value to current and potential employers. Above all, you will need to extract every last ounce of knowledge that you can from the resources the business school has to offer, and then learn to manage and use that knowledge as effectively as possible.

These are deep principles. It will be easy to lose sight of them in the day-to-day grind of courses and cases, and this indeed is one of the reasons why in Chapter 10 this book recommends ensuring a proper social life, giving a chance to not only do a little extra networking but also to relax and unwind. But the principles must be kept in sight. Do whatever you need to make sure this happens; write them on the wall of your study or office, put them on your screensaver, repeat them while brushing your teeth in the morning (try to avoid becoming boring in the presence of colleagues and family members, however).

The effort required is great. The rewards, for the successful, are greater still. Make sure that your MBA provides the maximum value it can for you.

ON THE WHOLE IT WAS WORTH
ALL THE STUDY

Index